Flowers That Last

PAULINE MANN

Flowers That Last

ARRANGING DRIED AND PRESERVED PLANTS & FLOWERS

B T BATSFORD LTD · *LONDON*

For all my flower-arranging friends

ISBN 0 7134 3842 8

Typeset by Keyspools Ltd, Golborne, Lancs
and printed in Great Britain by
R. J. Acford
Chichester, Sussex
for the publishers
B. T. Batsford Ltd.
4 Fitzhardinge Street
London W1H 0AH

Frontispiece: This attractive arrangement in a
stoneware container was designed using the
minimum of plant material in order to give a clear-
cut appearance and a feeling of space. It includes
Nicandra physaloides (shoo-fly plant), *Mahonia
japonica*, glycerined hostas, water plantain and
flowers made of wood shavings and teasels
Arranger: Janet Hayton

Contents

List of Arrangers & Photographers

Colour photographs

Black and white photographs

47	Janet Hayton	Derick Bonsall
50	Elizabeth Duffield	Derick Bonsall
52	Daphne Vagg	John Vagg
54	Adele Gotobed	Peter Harding
57	Vivien Armstrong	Derick Bonsall
60	Pauline Mann	Derick Bonsall
63	Pauline Mann	Derick Bonsall
64/5	Pauline Mann	Derick Bonsall
68	Pauline Mann	Derick Bonsall
67	Vera Bishop	John Vagg
69	Daphne Vagg	John Vagg
75	Alethia Chivers	Peter Chivers
76	Beryl Gray	Derick Bonsall
79	Pauline Mann	Derick Bonsall
83	Pauline Mann	Derick Bonsall
85	Susan Julian	Derick Bonsall
86	Mary Patterson	Derick Bonsall
89	Mollie Howgate	Derick Bonsall
91	Pauline Mann	Derick Bonsall
96	Daphne Vagg	John Vagg
97	Sheila Addinall	Derick Bonsall
100	Beryl Grisdale	Derick Bonsall
101	Mollie Howgate	Derick Bonsall
103	Pauline Mann	Derick Bonsall
104	Joyce Monks	Derick Bonsall
108	Joyce Monks	Derick Bonsall
110	Dorothy Hudson	Derick Bonsall
113	Winifred Simpson	James A. Fenmore
115	Elaine Fenwick	Derick Bonsall
119	Freda Hart	Jeremy Hall
122	Joyce Monks	Derick Bonsall
123	Inge Hanford	Derick Bonsall
125	Pauline Mann	Derick Bonsall
127	Pauline Mann	Derick Bonsall
128	Margaret Noble	Derick Bonsall
130	Dorothy Gray	Derick Bonsall
131	Pauline Mann	Derick Bonsall
133	Pauline Mann	Derick Bonsall
134	Pauline Mann	Derick Bonsall
137	Pauline Mann	Derick Bonsall

Acknowledgement

My very special thanks to Wendy Goodwill N.D.D., D.A.(Manc.) A.T.D., Lecturer in Art, York College of Arts and Technology, for doing the drawings and to Derick Bonsall A.R.P.S. for taking most of the photographs. I am indebted to all the flower arrangers who came to my house and put up designs to illustrate certain points. I am also grateful to Challis Garden Centre, York, for their co-operation.

Unless otherwise acknowledged in the captions the arrangements are by the author and the photographs by Derick Bonsall.

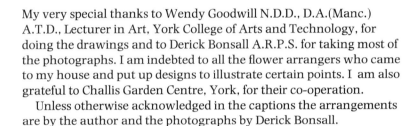

Note

It is illegal to uproot any wild plant; certain plants are protected by law and should not be picked. These are: Alpine gentian, Alpine snow thistle, saxifrage, ghost orchid, Killarney fern, lady's slipper, *Daphne mezereon*, Snowdon lily, spiked speedwell, spring gentian, Teesdale sandwort, tufted saxifrage and wild gladiolus.

Introduction

This book is for everyone who finds pleasure in some, if not all, aspects of flower arranging. It is also for the rushed host or hostess who wants an instant decoration which may be used several times, with simple variations.

Most flower arrangers have gardens and enjoy collecting and preserving plant material, but there are sources of supply for the gardenless too, for much can be found in the countryside, especially in the autumn. The sales tables of flower clubs, market stalls and florists' shops are aware of the demand for materials for preservation and do their best to meet the need. The skills of pressing, glycerining, skeletonizing and drying are extensions of the art of flower arranging and although fresh flowers can never fully be replaced, collage, picture making and the creation of dried decorations have a charm of their own. It is through these that we enjoy nature in retrospect.

Everyone wants their home to look attractive and possess the lively quality that flowers give to the surroundings. Central heating is hard on cut flowers; a dried or otherwise preserved arrangement will not wilt in a few days as cut flowers do. Fresh flowers are expensive for those who have no garden and may have to be a luxury to be indulged in only on very special occasions. The revival of interest in the methods of preservation reflects all these points. But there is another side to this: collage, the use of paints, silk flowers, wiring and pressing are crafts and are an outlet for creativity. Many find great relaxation in working with their hands to make pictures, plaques and garlands as well as less conventional decorations.

I suspect that when we ask for 'lasting arrangements' we are not thinking of the dusty assortment of honesty and teasles which used to stay in position from one November to the next, but have in mind a selection of well chosen pieces of plant material versatile enough to give distinction to two or three special flowers, fresh, handmade or silk.

I have taken each type of preservation separately, pointed out the

Arranger: Beryl Gray

advantages and limitations, and listed a selection of suitable plant material for use in that method and where to find it. Next I have described and explained each method of preservation. It is impossible to name everything that can be dried and glycerined, and anyway, experimenting is half the fun. The illustrations give some idea of how the end product can be assembled with the rhythm of the seasons in mind; for who wants fir cones at mid-summer?

NAFAS

The National Association of Flower Arrangement Societies (NAFAS) was founded in 1959 to encourage the love of flowers and to demonstrate their decorative value in the home.

The movement has met with spectacular success and there are now clubs all over Great Britain and Northern Ireland with over 100,000 individual members; there are many overseas affiliates. The society has provided an outlet for creativity for thousands of women and many men. It is now both an artistic and educational organization, working to promote a wider interest in flower arranging, gardening and the knowledge of plants. Money is raised for numerous charities at festivals and events and in 20 years the figure has reached £2 million.

NAFAS has its own trained and tested demonstrators, lecturers and judges, and its own handbook of schedule definitions for those who wish to enter competitive shows. Information regarding clubs in your area may be obtained from the Secretary, 21a Denbigh Street, London SW1V 2HF; please enclose a stamped addressed envelope.

1

Design

Flower arranging is an art form that has been practised for more than 4000 years. During this time there has not been just one style or one criterion of perfection; every civilization has had its own artists and craftsmen who have created in stone, wood and paint, leaving behind lasting examples of their skills which reflect changing fashion as well as geographical, economic and cultural differences. The walls of ancient Egyptian tombs had flowers carved upon them; Greek sarcophagi were festooned with fruit and flowers and the Corinthian column is still recognized by its acanthus leaves. The illuminated manuscripts of the early Christian church were exquisitely decorated with designs that included flowers. The cathedral masons and wood-carvers chiselled leaves, flowers and fruit on pillar capital, misericord and reredos. In Renaissance paintings the flowers used as symbols of the Virgin Mary and the Christian faith were depicted in scenes of the Holy Family. Later the Dutch-Flemish school of the sixteenth–seventeenth centuries made flowers the main subject of their paintings. Flowers always have, and still do, accompany mankind through life.

All creative people have in common the irrepressible urge to make something. The medium employed differs and the style changes from generation to generation but two things remain constant: the elements and principles of design. The elements of design are the working qualities, the actual physical components found in every composition, i.e. line, form, colour, texture and space. In this chapter I have outlined the basic principles of design and briefly described the elements. These are applicable to all types of flower arranging, whether of preserved or fresh material. Details of the particular relevance of the theories to dried and preserved flowers, leaves and seed heads will be found in the chapters on the various methods of preserving.

The flower arranger's material is produced by nature and needs only to be appreciated and selected. It is a wonderful living medium

and should be respected and used in a manner which acknowledges the characteristics of the many different plants. The flower arranger may feel he or she needs some guidance in combining these natural materials. Although the requirements for a pleasing arrangement are the same for preserved plant material as for fresh, the skill needed is perhaps greater when using dried and glycerined plants, as the lack of life must be compensated for by compelling design which may, if wished, last quite a long time – in the case of pictures, for decades. The basic laws of design provide this guidance and the principles of balance, rhythm, dominance, contrast, scale and proportion are as important a common bond between artists as are the elements or working qualitites. They are necessary to every art form and have provided the measuring rod for assessing a work of art for thousands of years. These laws are in no way restricting; they point the way and are guidelines to success.

Elements of Design

Line and Form

These two elements have much in common, as they both refer to and define shapes. Line, however, moves the eye, whereas form holds it. It is a combination of the two that produces the most pleasing effects.

Line

A line is a long, narrow shape which may be rounded, flat, gently curving, curly, zigzag, thick or thin, but in order to apprehend it the eye must move along the entire length from top to bottom or from left to right. Line makes movement and this is vital for the creation of rhythm and liveliness in any design.

An unbroken line is known as a *direct line* and a broken, but repetitive, line as an *indirect line*.

Line material is the flower arrangers' term which covers everything chosen to make a direct line. It includes a vastly differing range of plant material from dainty curving branches such as escallonia, selected by an arranger to move the eye to the extremities of a traditional pedestal, to the stark effect created by the stiff leaves of *phormium tenax* or sansevieria. Arcs of broom and spikes of flowers such as delphinium, foxglove and gladiolus are all in the line material category.

An arrangement illustrating the use of lines and circles in design. I have tried to capture the ethereal quality of dried hogweed by using a glass jug as a container and a double perspex base. The shiny honesty 'pennies' are in balls of dry foam

Direct (left) and indirect line

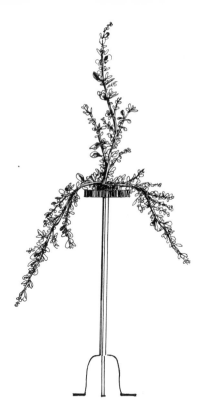

Line material: escallonia for a
traditional pedestal

Line material: arcs of broom

Spike of delphinium

Gladiolus

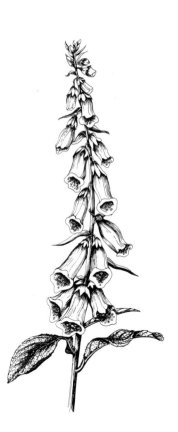

Foxglo

A round single flower with a
centre is very compelling

Flowers with trumpets are
volumetric, i.e. they contain space

All flowers are three-dimensional,
but this is particularly apparent
when they are seen from the side

Form

Unlike line, which moves the eye, form compels the eye to linger
upon it; the eye may move around the edge of the shape but there is
nothing to lead it away. Forms can be regular, irregular, flat, three-
dimensional or volumetric.

Many flowers are round in form and these attract the eye the
most. A round, single flower with a centre is very compelling.
Flowers with trumpets are of the volumetric type for they contain
space. All flowers are three-dimensional but especially so when seen
in profile. In flower arrangement round blooms have come to be
called 'points', meaning points of interest or points of importance.

17

Transitional forms

Traditional Western arrangements

These have their roots in the Dutch-Flemish flower pictures of
1600–1800. They depend upon a large number of massed flowers,
together with foliage of differing leaf size, for their impact. There is
little space, if any, within the design and the total effect is one of
abundance. The largest points are used towards the centre of the
arrangement, usually about one-third above the rim of the
container. The plant material used for direct line will frame the
perimeter of the arrangement and between the outline and the
central heart are many intermediate shapes; these are the
transitional materials, the links between the points and the line
material. The use of transitional items is a feature of traditional
design.

Another characteristic of the traditional mass arrangement is that
it fits into an imaginary geometric framework. The geometric shapes
for arrangements are the symmetrical and asymmetrical triangles,
the Hogarth curve, which is a double curve or 'lazy' S, the single
curve or crescent, the vertical, the diagonal and the oval. Amongst
these the triangle has become the most overworked. It is easy to
understand why it is so popular. It is a dignified and well balanced
structure, tapering as it does from a good firm base to a thin top.

Modern line arrangements

These can also have an imaginary geometric outline, but their
similarity with the traditional mass design stops here: modern line
arrangements reflect the sparseness and restraint seen in present-
day architecture and interior decoration. All transitional plant
material is omitted and the pieces used must be bold and clearly seen
in space.

Free form or free style

Designs in this style have no geometric framework. They depend
entirely for their shape upon the natural beauty of the plant material
used.

Colour

The appreciation of colour is entirely personal and tremendously
enjoyable. Women are usually interested and clever at using colour
in their homes and in their dress. It is a wide area and there is no
universally recognized theory on the subject. It is not necessary for
the flower arranger to delve deeply into theories of the refraction of
light, but there is a language of colour which helps to explain its
variations. Remember that colour is not constant, but is changed by
light and by other colours in juxtaposition.

Transitional material omitted from
a modern line arrangement

The terms used to describe the distinctive measurements of colour are:

Hue, which is used to differentiate between colours, e.g. red from blue; green from violet; and

Value, which refers to the lightness or darkness of a hue and is obtained by adding:

❊   White for a tint

❊   Grey for a tone

❊   Black for a shade

Chroma

Chroma is the word used to describe the measurement of the strength or weakness of a hue. Pure undiluted hues have maximum strength or saturation.

Neutral colours

The neutral colours are grey, black and white. These are also called achromatic colours, as they do not appear in the rainbow. The rainbow colours of red, orange, yellow, green, blue, indigo and violet are chromatic colours.

Monochromatic colouring

This refers to the tints, tones and shades of one colour. Dried and glycerined materials tend to be monochromatic.

Polychromatic colours

Polychromatic means containing many colours. The Dutch-Flemish school of painting in the sixteenth and following two centuries used polychromatic colouring.

Complementary colours

Complementary colours lie approximately opposite each other in the 'colour wheel' (see page 20): red-green, blue-orange, yellow-violet. Each supplies what the other lacks and therefore they accentuate each other.

Triadic colours

Triadic colours are any three equidistant hues on the colour wheel. The three primary colours, red, blue and yellow, are triadic.

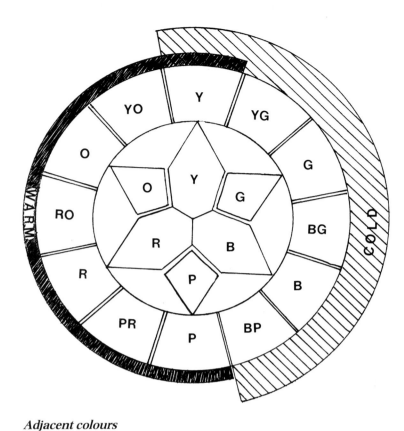

Colour circle

Y = yellow

G = green

B = blue

P = purple

R = red

O = orange

Adjacent colours

These lie next to each other on the wheel. They are harmonious and have a hue in common, e.g. red-orange, red and red-violet.

Colour temperature

Colours are warm or cool and some people are immensely affected by this factor. Greens and blues are on the cold side of the circle and reds and oranges on the warm side. In hospitals and nursing homes cool colours are used for decoration because they have a calming effect on the patients. Hot colours are known to excite and to increase the heart rate. Colour temperature is important to the flower arranger in interpretative designs.

Luminosity

This relates to the visibility of a colour in poor light. An excellent test for luminosity is to select flowers of various hues and of differing values of lightness and darkness. Take these into a dark room, then light a candle and see which flowers show up the best. White and tints (hues containing white) have high luminosity and the chromatic colours of yellow, orange and yellow-green, in that order,

OPPOSITE This arrangement has distinctive textures and a subtle colouring of cream, biscuit and pale coral. The tangly material is *gusano de oro* and the poppies are silk
Arranger: Geraldine Hazell

come next. Violet, blue-violet and blue vanish in dark surroundings and at a distance.

Flower arrangers often work in churches and cathedrals where the light is dim and they should bear in mind the luminosity of the flowers they use. White flowers mixed with others of a strong chroma stand out too obtrusively and look 'dotted' about. White is beautiful alone or with tints.

Visual weight

Colour has visual 'weight'. White and all tints are lighter than tones, and shades are heavy. The weight of pure hues varies; yellow is lighter than violet; red is lighter than blue. The flower arranger needs to understand the visual weight of colour, for its incorrect use will upset the balance of a design.

Texture

Texture may be appreciated by both sight and touch. It is the surface quality of any natural or man-made object. This element has increased in importance in recent years and has taken the place of more detailed and elaborate surface decoration in art. Interior designers, sculptors, architects and potters are especially aware of the interest a tactile surface gives to otherwise completely plain areas.

The value of texture in flower arranging cannot be over-estimated. The use of different textures gives contrast, and a feeling of rhythm can be created by deftly repeating a shiny texture throughout an arrangement. It also has an evocative quality, with downy surfaces conjuring up cosy feelings of warmth and scratchy ones suggesting discomfort. Shininess is associated with sophistication, silkiness with femininity, roughness with masculinity and so on. This element is therefore useful in interpretative work, i.e. arranging to a theme and trying to bring out the meaning of a title by using the colours, textures and shapes which it suggests.

It is a challenge to achieve contrast and interest in a dried design. Not only are so many dried items small but they can also have a dull texture. There are some ideas included in this book to help overcome these drawbacks, sometimes with the use of sprays, paints and dyes. But many people love the soft, subtle colouring of dried plant material and are quite happy with it as it is.

Space

Plenty of space, sea-fan, wood and *Eryngium tripartitum* give an underwater atmosphere to this unusual design
Arranger: Annette Dyson

Space is not tangible as the other design elements are, but only with space can line and form be seen at all. Flower arrangers are much more conscious of the importance of using space today than they

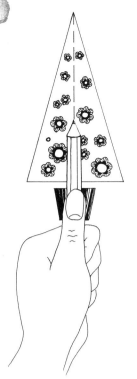

Hold a pencil in front of the eyes to check balance

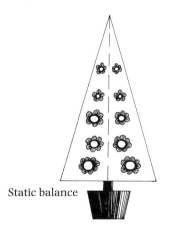

Static balance

The rhythmic repetition of circles here suggests dynamic force by the use of balanced space. The leek heads and hosta leaves, dried naturally, harmonize with the blue-grey ceramic container, which gives good visual weight to the arrangement
Arranger: Adele Gotobed
Photographer: Peter A. Harding

were a few years ago. In line arrangements, each piece of plant material has a far greater impact when surrounded by space. Enclosed space has visual weight and may be used to balance a solid form.

Think of the importance of a given working area, for example the show niche. The space available forms a background which enhances the exhibit. Nothing intrudes; the design will be framed by space. The exhibitor must use the space to advantage and neither underfill nor overfill it. The general rule is to take up two-thirds of the niche. It is the same with a collage, a picture, or with an arrangement in the home. Only when surrounded by space can forms be fully appreciated.

Principles of design

Balance

The flower arranger aims to have every design properly balanced in two ways:

❋ The arrangement must stand up firmly in whatever mechanics are best for the design.

❋ The arrangement must be visually balanced

Visual balance is equal eye attraction on each side of an imaginary vertical or horizontal line drawn through the middle of an arrangement. A simple aid to assessing whether the design is balanced is to hold a pencil in front of the eyes, close one eye and move the pencil to the centre of the design. Check that there is the same eye pull, visual weight and interest on each side. Different designs call for various kinds of balance.

Static balance

Flower arrangements are very often carried out within an imaginary framework. When this framework is equal each side of the vertical axis and both sides have identically placed plant material the balance created is motionless, brought about by identical attractions. Such static balance is not usually attempted by flower arrangers for there is little rhythm and it tends to be uninteresting. Certain pressed flower patterns may need static balance.

Symmetrical balance

Symmetrical balance is created when the framework on either side of

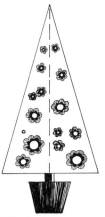

Symmetrical balance

the imaginary axis is identical but the plant material contained within the framework does not match. A far greater interest and more movement are gained by the differences. The eye-pull of both sides remains the same.

Dynamic balance

This is balance brought about by dissimilar attractions either side of the central axis; equal visual weight is given by the contrasting shapes. Dynamic balance is used in modern arrangements and is very effective because of its dramatic simplicity.

Asymmetrical balance

Asymmetrical balance has to be attained when the framework is unequal on each side of the axis and the materials used are also different. Landscapes, and any design with a double placement need asymmetrical balance because the second placement is always subsidiary and therefore different to the main arrangement.

Rhythm

Rhythm is a pattern of movement and rest and there are many ways of achieving it in flower arrangement. Rhythm must be an integral part of a design, and cannot be added later.

There are several different ways in which rhythm can be put into a design.

Dynamic balance

OPPOSITE The curvaceous horn container echoes the rhythmic use of *Hippophae rhamnoides* (sea buckthorn) in this design. The *Laurus nobilis* leaves are mounted into sprays. The other glycerined foliage is beech, box and ruscus. Some of the flowers are made of wood shavings and the others are dried grapefruit skins with cone centres
Arranger: Jo Thirlwall

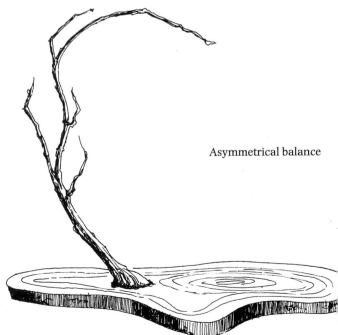

Asymmetrical balance

26

Rhythm achieved by radiation

❋   By the repetition of related lines and points throughout the design, causing the eye to follow the flow

❋   By the repetition of a hue

❋   By the repetition of a dominant texture

❋   By transition, i.e. by making gradual change from the focal point to the outline material.

❋   By radiation; most flower arrangements, unless they are abstract, radiate from one central point, in the same manner as a plant springs out of the ground.

Rhythm also helps in interpretation. Traditional subjects usually need gentle rhythmic patterns whilst modern and abstract interpretations will need more dynamic movement.

Dominance

In any design there must be some portions which are more important than others. In a flower arrangement it is essential to have points of emphasis, otherwise the resulting uniformity is uninteresting. In a traditional mass arrangement this does not mean one large, brightly coloured flower placed in a low central position which draws all eyes and holds them there. More often it is a lazy S of flowers, gently graduated in size and of an advancing colour, running in a broken line through the centre of the design. A smaller proportion of the dominant (i.e. large or brightly coloured) material is needed.

In abstract work several areas of greater interest may be created throughout the design, so there is more than one focal point. In modern arrangements dominance is easier to attain because of the dramatic quality of the plant material and the use of space.

It is always the plant material which should predominate, so aggressively coloured containers and bases, or accessories that are too obtrusive, are best left alone, especially for show work.

Contrast

In a mass arrangement contrast is not as easily noticeable as it is in modern and abstract designs. But there need to be differences of form and texture or the arrangement lacks spice. Gentle contrast is suited to traditional arrangements, but in line designs bold contrast can be used with striking results.

OPPOSITE The brown and cream ceramic container is geometrical with straight lines, space within its design and a puffed candy texture. Perhaps straight-lined plant material suggests itself but here curving lines have been used to accentuate the contrast between the plant material and the container. Dry foam inside the container holds the preserved winter branches of contorted hazel – *Corylus avellana* 'Contorta'. The round flower shape is fashioned from the cream, glycerined leaves (cladodes) of ruscus, the tips of which were touched with a rubber-based glue and pushed between the scales of a pine cone. The wide gaps between the scales of the pointed end of the cone conveniently grip the branches. The depth of colour and smoothness of the base are in contrast to the rough texture of the peach stones and the container
Arranger: Mattie Young
Photographer: Donald I. Innes

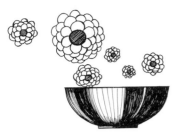

Sizes in relationship

Scale

Scale is the relationship of sizes. Nothing can be considered too big or too small or just right for size until it is seen in context. In flower arranging all the component parts must be in scale with one another and also with the position which the design is intended to grace. The container must be right for the setting; the base suitable for the container; the flowers and foliage in happy relationship with each other and the container. If accessories are used they should also be of the correct scale. Only then will harmony result.

Proportion

Proportion is concerned with amounts and not sizes. Everything used for an arrangement may be in scale but if too much plant material is put into the container, overwhelming it, then the proportion of plant material is excessive. It is possible for everything in a show niche to be in scale but for the niche to be filled so full that the proportion of design to working space is incorrect. Proportion relates to the height and width of the design also; the usual rough guide is that the tallest piece of material should be at least one and a half times the height or width, whichever is the greater measurement, of the container. This factor does depend on the type of plant material used and often the height needs to be more.

   The principle of proportion is involved in the choice of the relative amounts of colours for a design. Equal numbers of each hue tend to give a static appearance. A good rule is to use a smaller number of flowers of the most intense colour, and to avoid colours of a similar chroma.

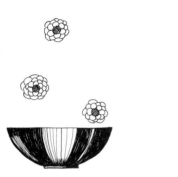

Correct scale but too few flowers

Correct scale but too many flowers

2

Pressing Flowers

Most of us have taken a book from a shelf in someone's house and on opening it have found a pressed flower; or while carrying out the sad task of sorting through old letters, have come across an unrecognizable papery flower amongst the written sheets. Perhaps pressed flowers suffer from sentimental associations, but there is something appealing in trying to capture moments of happiness or in keeping memories of people and places.

The revival of interest and enthusiasm for flower arranging has resulted in a fashion for preserving the bride's bouquet, either with a desiccant or by pressing, so that it can be re-assembled in the original form or as a picture. Girls sometimes choose silk flowers for their wedding bouquets because they can be kept as a memento. Pictures made from pressed flowers are often handed down from one generation to another and the Victorians especially indulged in the pastime of pressing flowers. It is a fascinating pursuit. Although you are limited to two dimensions, a third may be hinted at by careful overlapping of the plant material, and the picture will retain its colour, which is a great attraction, for some years; even when it fades, the beautiful silhouette of leaf and petal will remain. When material with depth is added, the design becomes a plaque or collage rather than a pressed flower picture.

Cards and calendars, as well as pictures, are simple to make; table mats, napkin rings and finger plates are other possibilities. Shops sell trinket boxes and dressing table accessories which can be decorated with flowers (see list of stockists, pages 140–1). Pressed material has the great advantage of being easy to store in a dry place and of taking up very little room.

32

Flower presses

There are various sizes of flower press on the market. These are made of two pieces of thick plywood, layers of corrugated paper and blotting paper. The sizes range from 13cm × 13cm to 25·5cm × 25·5cm (5½in × 5½in to 10in × 10in). Four bolts and four wing nuts clamp the boards, corrugated paper and blotting paper together to give a uniform pressure on the plant material.

It is perfectly simple to make a press out of two squares of 7-ply wood 25·5cm × 25·5cm (10in × 10in). Smooth the edges of the wood with sandpaper and then bore four holes 6mm (¼in) in diameter about 13mm (½in) from each corner in both pieces of wood. Insert four bolts, 6mm (2½in) long upwards through the bottom plywood. Cut ten or twelve pieces of corrugated card and double that number of pieces of blotting paper, cutting off the corners of both so that they fit inside the bolts. Fit the top on to the bolts and screw on the nuts.

Using a thick book as a press

Flowers press quite well inside blotting paper in the pages of a thick book, especially if the book is one of many on a shelf and so tightly held by others. Alternatively the book may be laid flat with bricks or other books on top of it to weigh it down. The results may not be quite as uniformly smooth as in a proper press, but this a good substitute.

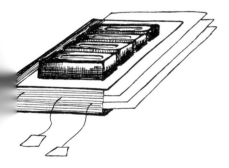

Using a thick book as a press

Another improvised press

An improvised press can be made out of a stack of old magazines and blotting paper. Top the pile with a piece of plywood or chipboard of similar size to the magazines and weigh this down with bricks. It is very easy to add another layer of flowers to this makeshift press without disturbing the flowers already there. Flowers may be transferred from the proper press to this improvised one after a few weeks, so freeing the more efficient one for a new batch.

This three-dimensional picture contains *briza media*, box, bracken, leather fern, eucalyptus, lycopodium, orgona, beech mast, cones, helichrysum and *Anaphalis yedoensis*
Arranger: Barbara Atkinson

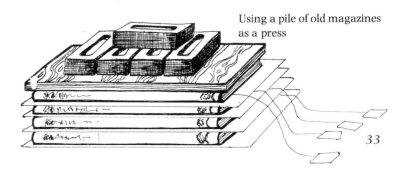

Using a pile of old magazines as a press

On the left are two ribboned pomanders and a book marker for the lectern for a church festival. The two cards are the work of Eileen Lambert and the paperweight was made by Elsie Bark. The beautifully decorated pomanders in the centre and the boxes and candle were made by Nan Shephard

Collecting and selecting plant material

As the object of pressing is the removal of moisture from the plant material, it is best to collect on a dry day and to get the flowers and leaves into the press quickly before they wilt. Plants with a high water content are not suitable for pressing. Choose undamaged specimens, for it is a waste of time and space to press imperfect ones.

When gathering flowers bear in mind all the possible styles of picture that can be made:

❊   A mass arrangement, with an imaginary outline of geometric shape

❊   A line arrangement, with plenty of space and movement in the design

❊   A landscape or scene

❊   An abstract, which will use the plant material for its design qualities and not naturalistically

Select as varied an assortment of flowers and foliage as possible and include plants at different stages of development. The outline of the material is of primary importance. Thin leaves and petals are the best and often the simplest flowers are the most pleasing and effective. The hedgerow will supply a wonderful selection.

Sources of supply

The countryside

If you have access to the countryside there is an abundance of material to be found for pressing. Even the verge of a country road is a good hunting ground. The plants listed below are favourites of mine and are chosen for the numerous leaf shapes and interesting growth habits. The flowers are mostly small; the buttercup, primrose and cranesbill are the largest I have mentioned. Remember, almost anything can be pressed if the guidelines are followed – the exceptions are succulents and very thick leaves and flowers.

A landscape picture containing (from the left on the skyline) three sections of red Japanese maple, a piece of rose root, two lemon-scented geranium leaves and an 'island' made of the underside of a raspberry leaf. The tree is an *Alchemilla mollis* leaf and the tall tree a potentilla stem; in front of it are white lamium leaves. In the foreground are oak, tulip stamens, moss, Solomon's seal, cherry and grass seeds. The background is hardboard treated with two coats of white paint. A clear adhesive was used
Arranger: Margaret Cash
Photographer: Stevenson Studios, County Down

Botanical name	Common name	Comments	Flowering time
Alchemilla mollis	Lady's mantle	Lime-green bracts	June
Anagallis	Pimpernel	Small, flat, scarlet, blue or white flowers	June–August
Anemone nemorosa	Wood anemone	Attractive leaves, white flowers	March–April
Anthriscus sylvestris	Cow parsley	Leaves and tiny flowers	May–June
Pteridium aquilinum	Bracken	Press any time. Colour good in autumn	Autumn
Bryonia dioica	Bryony	Small cream-green flowers, beautiful tendrils	July
Campanula rotundifolia	Harebell	Delicate blue flowers, fine stems and leaves	July–September
Dryas octopetala	—	Leaves and flowers	June–July
Euphorbia helioscopia	Sun spurge	Lime-green bracts	Early summer
Foeniculum vulgare	Fennel	Feathery foliage	July–October
Galanthus nivalis	Snowdrop	Flowers and leaves	January–March
Gallium	Bedstraw	A feathery plant; use entire stems	June–September
Geranium	Cranesbill	Simple flowers, excellent leaves	Summer
—	Grasses	Good line material	Summer
Linum usitatissimum	Common flax	Pale blue flowers	June–July
Lonicera	Honeysuckle	Tubular flowers and tendrils	Summer
Lotus corniculatus	Bird's foot trefoil	Leaves and flowers	June–August
Myosotis	Forget-me-not	Tiny blue, white or pink flowers	Spring
Oxalis acetosella	Wood sorrel	White flowers, beautiful leaves	April–May
Polygala vulgaris	Common milkwort	Very dainty flowers and foliage	May–August
Potentilla anserina	Silverweed	Yellow flower, soft grey leaf	July–August
Primula vulgaris	Primrose	Flowers, buds and leaves press well	February–May
Ranunculus	Buttercup – many species	Presses well	Spring–summer
Silene	Campion	White flowers with large, attractive calyces	Summer
Stellaria	Chickweed	Small and pretty	Summer
Thalictrum flavum	Common meadow rue	Yellow flowers and deep green foliage	June–July
Trifolium	Clover	Leaves	Summer
Veronica	Speedwell	Small blue flowers	Late spring–summer
Vicia	Vetch	Leaves and tendrils	Spring–summer
Vinca minor	Lesser periwinkle	Blue flowers	March–August
Viola canina	Dog violet	Flowers and foliage	Spring
Viola tricolour	Tricolour pansy	Flowers and leaves	April–September

The garden, nurseries and florists

Below is a list of easily cultivated alpine and border plants that press well. Those marked with an asterisk * are obtainable from market stalls, garden centres and shops.

Botanical name	Common name	Comments	Flowering time
Alchemilla alpina	—	Beautiful silver leaves	Summer
A. mollis	Lady's mantle	May be found in the wild or cultivated	Summer
Astilbe spp	—	Flowers with feathery plumes, dainty leaves	Summer
Aubretia	—	Rock plant. The scale is good for pictures even if the colour retention varies	Spring
Dianthus (single)	Pink	Keep their colour well. Many have fringed petals	May–June
Dryas octopetala	—	May also be found in the wild	June–July
Eurphorbia spp	—	Many cultivated varieties with red, yellow and bright green bracts	Spring–summer
Geranium	Cranesbill	Many alpine and border varieties. Simple flowers and interesting leaves	Summer
Geum	—	Simple flowers	Summer
Helianthemum	Rock rose	Pink, white, red and orange simple flowers	Summer
Hepatica	—	Small, blue flowers	Early spring
Heuchera sanguinea	Coral flower	Very attractive leaves. Small pink or red flowers	June–September
Hydrangea spp	—	Press single florets	Late summer
Lonicera spp	Honeysuckle	Many cultivated varieties provide tubular flowers	Summer
Montbretia	—	Curved tubular flowers	Late summer
Nepeta spp	Catmint	Grey-green leaves	May–July
Potentilla spp	—	Good for flowers and foliage	Summer
Primula auricula	—	Similar to the primrose in shape	Spring
P. polyanthus	—	As above	Spring
Rosa 'Nazomi'	—	Single miniature pink roses; small scale	June
Viola spp	—	All species press well	Continuous

The table of foliage plants give below lists those whose foliage I find particularly attractive. Those marked by an asterisk * can be bought easily in markets and shops. Some are houseplants.

Botanical name	Common name	Comments
Acer palmatum vars.	Japanese maple	Palmate leaves in reds and greens
—	*Ferns (various)	Fern fronds
Galanthus nivalis	Snowdrop	Leaves give straight, slender, line material
Hedera spp	Ivy	Small leaves are especially good
Helichrysum angustifolium	Curry plant	Small-leafed grey spikes
Lathyrus	Sweet pea	Tendrils
*Pelargonium	Geraniums (indoor)	*P. crispum* 'Variegatum' and other species which have leaf markings are especially good
Rosa spp	Rose	Beautiful foliage
Ruta graveolens	Rue	Glaucous foliage
Thymus spp	Thyme	Dainty foliage

Using a press

Cut off all flower stems and press separately. They may be curved and held in place with adhesive tape

❈   Be methodical and label each layer.

❈   Leaves and flowers may be placed quite close together, but must not touch. Use a soft paint brush and an orange stick to arrange the materials on the blotting paper.

❈   Cut off all flower stems and press separately. These may be curved and held in place with adhesive tape.

❈   Press open, flat flowers face downwards.

❈   Press buds and flowers in profile. Tubular flowers must be cut in half before they are pressed in profile. If a tubular flower is to be pressed 'full face' remove the tubular part. The centre will have to have a new middle given to it later.

Flower heads with florets

Flower heads with numerous florets, e.g. hydrangeas, delphinium and verbascum, need to have each tiny flower or bract dealt with individually.

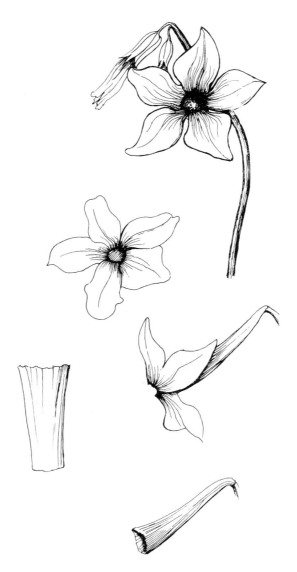

If a tubular flower is to be pressed 'full face', remove the tubular part

Double flowers

Many-petalled flowers must be dismantled, each petal pressed by itself and the whole later reassembled.

Flowers with elaborate centres

Single flowers which have complicated centres e.g. clematis, must have each petal-like sepal and each stamen taken apart, pressed and then put together again. Many people are skilled at this and it is simply a question of trial and error.

Closing the press

When all the pieces have been put between the blotting paper and corrugated card and labelled, close the press. Do this carefully so that nothing is dislodged. Avoid tightening the press to its maximum at first for this may damage very thin materials. Screw it a bit tighter each day until maximum pressure has been achieved.

Leave the press undisturbed for at least three weeks. Three months is even better. Do keep the press in a dry room.

Storing pressed flowers

When pressed material is ready to be moved, transfer the contents of the press very carefully on to more blotting paper. A small round-ended knife will be useful for lifting items which have got stuck, but if you gently curl the blotting paper in your hand the movement will nearly always release obstinate petals. Store the plant material in one of the improvised presses or in boxes, preferably in labelled layers and always on blotting paper; it must be stored flat and in a dry place.

Colour retention

In time most pressed flowers fade, but even then a picture can give pleasure, for the shapes remain outlined against the backing paper.

If you feel you want more colour than the pressed material has naturally and you have no objections to aiding nature, some flowers may be touched up with water-based paint. The surface of petals and leaves sometimes rejects water paint, but a drop of washing-up liquid mixed with the water will overcome this problem. Remember, though, that the painted flowers and leaves will retain their artificial colouring when the untreated pieces fade, so the merest suggestion of added colour is all that is needed.

When the flowers and leaves are pressed you will find:

Orange and yellow hold their colour best

Green fades to grey-green over a period of time

Grey remains constant

Red darkens to brown

Blue varies in different flowers but will tend to darken

Brown stays brown

Purple darkens

White also varies, sometimes going grey or cream.

Making a picture

Equipment

Press
Background paper
Mounting card
Frame
Rubber-based adhesive
Transparent adhesive
Brown sticky tape
Cardboard for backing
Scissors – curved and straight
Paint brush
Thin piece of wood, e.g. an orange stick
Tweezers
Eyelets and hanging cord
Small knife with rounded end

Choosing a frame

It is best to decide on the colour scheme and style of the picture before choosing a frame. The right frame makes all the difference and it is worth taking trouble to find it. Pressed flowers are delicate, almost ethereal, and can so easily be overwhelmed by too ornate or heavy a border.

An abstract design needs a plain, modern frame. A landscape or scene must not have a frame that distracts the viewer's eye from the picture. A mass design can take a more elaborate border, but it must not diminish the effect of the flowers.

Backing paper

Also of great importance is the colour of the background paper. Yellow, orange and tawny flowers will be enhanced by a coffee-coloured background. Pale green-grey used as a background is always a good choice, especially with pink and soft red plant material. Black is dramatic. Art shops will have various textures and colours to choose from, or you may want a fabric background. If you decide on the latter the fabric's texture must not be too dominant for the thin plant material. Fabric is perhaps better used either for a mount or for collage. If you want a mount it is easy to place it behind the background on to which the flowers have been glued. This ensures that the plant material will be held tightly against the glass of the frame. If the picture is recessed into a cut-out mount that holds

the flowers away from the glass, the plant material may curl away from its backing.

Shops sell good selections of frames for pictures and some have very thin paper mounts which are very attractive. Box frames and recessed mounts for three-dimensional pictures are also available.

Starting the picture

Cut the background paper to the same size as the frame and also cut some cardboard to pad out the back. The picture must be tight against the glass. This not only helps to keep the material flat but excludes air and so prolongs the colour life of the picture.

Have two identical pieces of the chosen backing paper in front of you, cut to the right size, and try out the design on one of them. The tweezers, paint brush, knife and orange stick will help you to position the flowers. The rules of design apply to picture making as much as to any other kind of flower arrangement, so give the design movement, contrast in texture and form, making sure it is balanced and that all the components are in scale with the frame and one another. Try not to fill the frame more than two-thirds full; for many styles more space is necessary. Also, leave a slightly wider margin at the bottom of a picture than at the top, otherwise the picture seems to be falling out of the frame.

Fixing the plant material

When you are quite satisfied with the way the plant material is placed on the trial card, transfer it piece by piece, sticking it as you go, to the permanent background. It is best to work from the top downwards to avoid brushing your hand against the things already fixed, but it is also helpful to put in certain key pieces first to establish the width and height of the design. Use rubber-based glue, either on a brush or an orange stick, touching each petal and leaf lightly as you hold them in the tweezers. If a leaf is long dab it with glue in more than one place. If water paint has been used on any items more glue will be needed, for the paint makes them brittle. Use a clean tissue to press a flower if necessary.

The four seasons fill the ovals of the pale green velvet frame on the left. The daisies in the top right pressed picture have a blue background and a thin superimposed mount. The design in the oval frame at the bottom is of leaves only, in shades of green, autumn reds and browns

Finishing

Leave the picture to dry thoroughly for three or four days, and make sure the glass is clean and shining before enclosing the picture in its frame. Use panel pins to get the back of the frame really firm. The back can be finished neatly with brown paper stuck down with rubber-based glue or brown adhesive tape. You will need eye screws and nylon cord for hanging.

You may like to sign your name on the picture and put a list of flowers used on the back of the frame, along with the date.

Four ways of pressing large leaves

✳   Large leaves may be pressed in blotting paper and placed in a book or under the carpet. If they are put under the carpet give them the added protection of a layer of newspaper. Bracken is best pressed this way; it is so bulky and the stems are too big to be contained in a book. It helps to prevent the material from cracking if a little oil is brushed over the surface before pressing. The leaves can be wired singly after treatment or grouped into sprays.

✳   Try dipping leaves into melted paraffin wax, then put them between newspaper and iron them at the heat suited to synthetic fabrics.

✳   Put the leaves between newspaper and use a warm iron to press them for about five minutes. The colour retention will be good though the leaves may not last as well as those treated by the slow pressing method.

✳   Place the leaves between sheets of waxed paper and using a warm iron press them carefully for a few minutes. Then shut them in a book, still in the waxed paper, for 48 hours.

Some suitable leaves for these treatments are:
Crocosmia
Gladiolus
Iris
Maple
Prunus

Finger plates

You can buy transparent plastic plates to protect the paint from finger marks and use pressed flowers to decorate them.

✳   Cut the card to fit under the plate.

✳✳   Cover the card with thin fabric and either tape or glue the raw edges of the fabric to the back of the card.

✳✳✳   Place the flowers on the card and when you are satisfied with the design glue them on with rubber-based glue.

✳✳✳✳ Put the decorated card into the door plate and fix it to the door.

Greetings cards

A frame gives a pressed picture its professional finish and the mounting card acts as a frame when making a greetings card. It needs to be without blemish.

There is a good choice of coloured and white mounting cards to be had in art shops, and it can be cut to any size with the aid of a guillotine. Bear in mind the guidelines for any design and match the scale of the flowers to the size of the mount and their colour to the background.

A three-fold card enables you to have a framed front and gives you an area of card for the design which will, on completion, fill the frame. The third fold allows the open card to stand firmly.

There are many places which sell ready-made cards in various sizes and a selection of colours. There is much to recommend them, especially for the beginner. The addresses of stockists are given at the back of the book (pages 140–1).

Whether the card is ready-made or home-made, a protective film is necessary to cover the pressed flowers. This film is obtainable from a stationer. Many of the ready-made cards are supplied together with protective film.

3

Drying Plant Material

Drying is probably the most widely practised method of preserving flowers and seed heads for winter decoration. It is simple to carry out and no special equipment is needed. Materials are easy to come by even for those who have no garden.

A well illustrated seedsman's catalogue is a tremendous help. This has sections for the flower arranger, and the instructions about seed sowing along with the photographs of the end results give all the necessary information.

The three main sources of supply of plant material for drying are:

❊ The garden

❊ The countryside

❊ Market stalls, florists' shops and garden centres

The garden

'Everlasting' flowers

There are some 'everlasting' flowers which the French call *immortelles*; these are papery to the touch and straw-like; indeed one of the group, the helichrysum, is known as the straw-flower. Most of these are half-hardy or hardy annuals with the exception of anaphalis and some of the statice species which are perennials. The *immortelles* have small flowers, some quite tiny, but they do retain their colour for several years.

Tie the bundles to a line of some
sort or to a coathanger

The Victorians loved hand vases
and this one would be just right for
the guest room. The formal oval
posy is of helipterums,
helichrysums and grasses
Arranger: Elizabeth Duffield

Picking and drying 'Everlasting' flowers

Gather the flowers before they are wide open, and always on a dry
day. They will continue to mature as they dry. Pick some in bud too
so that there is a selection of sizes. Some stems may be strong enough
to support the flower when the time comes to arrange it, but among
the small annuals and half-hardy annuals the majority will need
wiring (see page 90). The leaves will wither and have to be taken off
eventually.

Prepare them in the following way:

❊   Remove all leaves,

❊❊   Bunch the flowers in small numbers and tie tightly; as they
dry they will contract and the flowers will drop out if they are not
well secured.

❊❊❊   Hang the bunches upside down. This ensures that the top
of the stem and the head remain straight and firm. A centimetre
($\frac{1}{2}$in) of stem near the head of the flower will be needed if they are to
be wired later.

❊❊❊❊   Tie the bundles to a line of some kind or to a coat
hanger, rows of nails or a clothes horse in an airy position.

The colour will be better if the bunches are hung in a dimly lit place.
The length of time taken for drying depends upon the weather,
density of the flower heads and stage of development.

The following table gives details of some frequently used
'everlasting' flowers.

Botanical name	Common name	Comments	Flowering time
Acroclinium roseum	—	Pale pink and rose-pink daisies	June–July. H.a.
Ammobium alatum	—	Silvery-white petals, yellow centres	July–October
Anaphalis	Pearl everlasting	Small, fluffy, white flowers	Late summer. H.p.
Helichrysum bracteatum	Straw flowers	Good range of varieties	July–first frost. H.h.a.
Helipterum manglesii	Rhodanthe	Rose and silvery-white daisies	June–July. H.a.
Limonium dumosum	Statice	Small white flowers, good shape	July–August. H.p.
L. sinuatum	Statice	Varied colours: blue, yellow, rose, pink, lavender and white	Late July–September. H.h.a.
L. suworowii	Statice	Rose-pink plume-shaped panicles	July–September. H.h.a.
Xeranthemum	—	Wiry-stemmed daisies: white, pink, rose and lilac	June–August. H.a.

H.a. Hardy annual
H.h.a. Half-hardy annual
H.p. Hardy perennial

Bottles of varying greens and a
pepper mill here provide the
vertical accent often lacking in
table settings. Colourful yellow,
green and cream gourds are
casually grouped with several
dried heads of artichoke on a
hessian-covered two-tier base
Arranger Daphne Vagg
Photographer: John Vagg

Other garden plants

Other garden material includes annuals, biennials, half-hardy annuals and some sub-shrubs. It is a large group containing the familiar shapes that have always been seen in dried arrangements. The greater proportion of these are dried as seed heads, though some are gathered in flower. I have described the stage of development at which a flower should be picked in the plant list. Nearly all the plants in this category are easy to come by and simple to grow.

Delphiniums and larkspur can be dried in flower but remember to gather the spikes just before the top flowers mature. If there is no dimly lit, airy place in which to hang them, try enclosing the spikes in brown paper bags to protect them from the light. Make a few holes in the bags so that some air gets in. Another way it put the flowers into the airing cupboard.

Seed heads are best left to dry on the plant – this is, after all, what nature intended; but avoid leaving them too long once they have ripened in case they are spoilt by bad weather.

Gourds, artichokes and cardoons need to be dried in full sunshine or in a very warm airing cupboard. Gourds take a long time (at least three months) and when they are ready they feel light and empty. They may then be protected with a coat of varnish.

Most people find hydrangeas and achilleas dry satisfactorily if they are defoliated and then placed in 5cm (2in) of water. Keep them in a warm place until the water has been taken up and then hang them upside down and finish the drying process as for other flowers. I have never had very good results from this method with hydrangeas and recently I tried another way which has been much more satisfactory. Success depends on gathering the heads at exactly the right time, when they feel crisp to the touch. Dry them quickly near a radiator or boiler without putting them in water. They do seem to keep their colour extremely well this way.

Hydrangeas provide one of the largest round forms for dried arrangements to be found in the English garden and are therefore invaluable. The blues dry with wonderfully subtle colouring. They may also be bleached or sprayed sparingly with car spray. The individual fresh florets press beautifully for pictures and are useful for collage. They take oil and water-based paint equally well.

Broom, cane and certain other more unusual dried materials from overseas can be tied into curves or special shapes and left in water overnight. They must then be dried before being untied, so that they will keep their new contour.

OVERLEAF This arrangement was designed to complement the picture in texture and colour. The colours used are beige, yellow, orange, red, brown and green. The design features millet, wheat, oats and delphinium seed heads together with physalis (chinese lanterns), gourds of various shapes and dried red chillies; glycerined laurel leaves add another texture. A green Wedgwood fruit dish enhances the plant material
Arranger: Adele Gotobed

54

Annuals and hardy perennials

Botanical name	Common name	Comments	Flowering time
Acanthus spinosus	Tall spikes	Dry when seeds are forming	August–September. H.p.
Achillea spp	—	Flat heads or small flowers: yellow, cream, white. Stand in water	August–September. H.p.
Alchemilla mollis	Lady's mantle	Lime-green feathery bracts. Hang in bunches upside down	Late June–July. H.p.
Allium porrum	Leek	Large onion-like heads	Autumn
Amaranthus caudatus	Love-lies-bleeding	Red and green tassels. A new variety is a mixture of green, orange-yellow and bronze	August–September. H.h.a.
Aquilegia	Columbine	Dry the seed heads	May–June. H.p.
Araucaria araucana	Monkey puzzle	Dried branches provide leaves for collage and textured stems for modern designs	Evergreen
Artemisia ludoviciana	White sage	Silver-grey leaves	July–first frost. H.p.
Astrantia major	Masterwort	Green-pink flushed flowers	Early summer. H.p.
Ballota pseudo-dictamnus	—	Remove leaves before drying: whorls of green 'felt' remain	July–first frost
Carlina acaulis	—	Dry in full flower	July. H.p.
Cynara cardunculus	Cardoon	Pick and dry in heat when in full flower	H.p.
C. scolymus	Globe artichoke	As above	H.p.
Delphinium consolida	Larkspur	Blue, pink and white spikes	June–July. H.a.
Dryas octopetala	—	Fluffy white seed heads. Leave on plant to dry	H.p.
Gomphrena globosa	Globe amaranth	Dry the clover-like flower	July–September. H.h.a.
—	Grasses	—	Summer
—	Gourd	Sow in full sun; dry in heat	July–September. H.h.a.
Hydrangea	—	Pick the flower heads when they feel crisp to the touch	September–October. P.
Iris foetidissima	—	Brilliant orange seeds. Spray with a fixative	September–October. P.
Limonium incarnum	Statice	Small flowers which give a cloudy effect	June–August. H.p.
L. latifolium	Blue-cloud statice	—	July–September. H.p.
L. suworowii	—	Rose-pink, plume-shaped panicles	July–September. H.h.a.
Lunaria annua	Honesty	Gather the stems of seed pods when they begin to dry	July–August. B.
Molucella laevis	Bells of Ireland	The green bracts will turn to cream when dried. Brittle	August. H.h.a.
Nicandra	Shoo-fly	Papery lanterns	September. H.a.

Annuals and hardy perennials continued

Nigella damascena	Love-in-a-mist	Attractive large seed heads	August. H.a.
Papaver somniferum	Poppy	The best seed heads for drying	July–August. H.a.
Physalis franchettii	Chinese lanterns	Dry by hanging	September. H.p.
Phytolacca americana	Poke wood	Dry by hanging	June–September
Scabiosa stellata 'Drumstick'	Scabious	Burnished bronze seed heads	July–August. H.a.
Stachys lanata	Lamb's ears	Grey spikes; remove leaves	July–August. P.
Zea	Ornamental corn	Interesting new varieties available	August–September. H.h.a.

Bulbs

Botanical name	Common name	Comments	Picking time
Allium spp	—	Allow umbels to dry on the plant	Throughout summer, depending on species
Camassia	Quamash lily	Spikes of cream seed pods	July
Crocosmia	—	Brown seed heads	September
Fritillaria imperialis	Crown Imperial	Splendid cream seed heads	September
Lilium martagon	Turk's cap lily	Good seed heads	August
Muscari	Grape hyacinth	Small, spiky seed heads	Spring

All cones are collectable

Alder cones

The countryside

The late summer and autumn will naturally yield the best supplies.

Most members of the Umbelliferae family have attractive seed heads. Among these is the giant hogweed which is so pleasing for modern and abstract designs, both its stems and the umbrella-like spokes. However, a word of caution about hogweed: the media keep issuing warnings of the dangers of touching it without protective gloves, for it gives some people a rash. When it has dried out thoroughly it is safe to handle, but it is also invasive and care should be taken not to spread the seeds. It is easy to cut off the seeds and place them in a newspaper so that they can be destroyed.

In the late summer and autumn it is more a question of what not to gather than otherwise – there is so much to choose from. Wheat, barley and rye must be obtained before harvest time, and grasses collected before they get spoilt by damp autumn weather. *Equisetum telmateia* is fascinating when dried and makes good line material. All cones are collectable, from the small alder cones upwards in size to the large spruce and cedar. Dock, old man's beard, lichened wood,

Pine cone

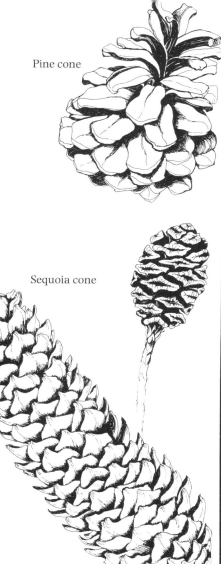

Sequoia cone

Spruce cone

A hogweed Christmas tree on a
1·5 metre (5 foot) bamboo cane
(dowelling would do just as well).
It is set in a pot of plaster and the
graduated sections of hogweed
stem have the right diameter holes
made through them with a
screwdriver so that they will slot
on to the central stem. They can be
swivelled to get some variation of
direction. The tree may be sprayed
or glittered and decorated with
baubles. It will fold flat for storage
Arranger: Vivien Armstrong

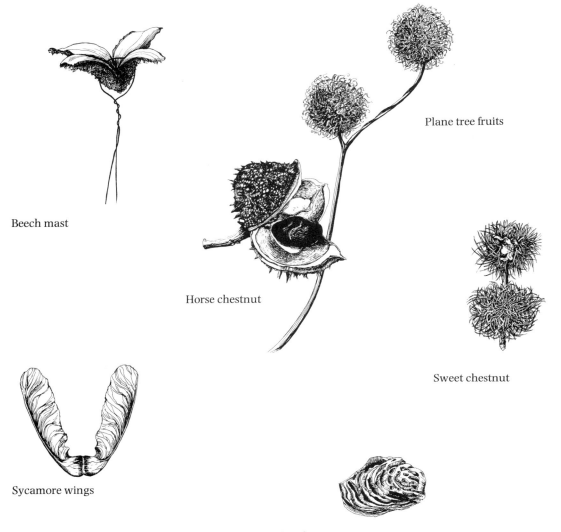

Beech mast

Plane tree fruits

Horse chestnut

Sweet chestnut

Sycamore wings

Peach stone

rose-bay willow herb and foxgloves should be harvested, dried off and sprayed with a fixative. Pick up beech mast, sycamore wings, plane tree fruits, horse chestnuts, sweet chestnuts and acorns. They can be used for collage, wired into swags and garlands and made into Christmas decorations. Before storing any of these make sure they are clean.

The following table lists some of the material available in the countryside:

Botanical name	Common name	Comments	Picking time
Anthriscus sylvestris	Cow parsley	Umbrella-like-spokes. Fragile	July–August
Brassica napus	Rape	Strong, creamy seed heads	July
Chamaenerion angustifolium	Rose-bay willow herb	Pick at seeding stage. Spray with fixative	July–September
Equisetum telmateia	Giant horse tail	Remove leaves after drying	September–October
—	Grasses	—	Summer
Heracleum sphondylium	Hogweed	Giant umbrella-like spokes. Always destroy seeds. Useful stems	July–August
Pteridium aquilinum	Bracken or brake	Gather when turning colour. Press between thick paper under carpet.	September–October
Rumex longifolius	Dock	Brown spikes. Gather assorted colours	August–September
Typha latifolia	Great reedmace (Bullrush)	—	June–August
Zea	Maize	Many varieties for flower arrangers	August–September

Market stalls, florists' shops and garden centres

It is worth while looking to see if the market stalls have any of the little everlasting flowers. Over the last decade the demand has increased so much that these are now grown by many nurserymen. They will cut all the crop when it is ready and bunch the whole plant. You will have to prepare them yourself for drying. The first to be ready in this group are the acrocliniums and rhodanthe which sometimes appear at the beginning of July or even earlier in the south of England. The helichrysums come later, in August and September. Florists' shops and garden centres usually have stocks of these flowers too but they will sell them later in the season, probably dried and costing so much each. It is always a good idea to ask for the other flowers named on page 51. There will certainly be physalis and a number of grasses, including pampas grass, many of them dyed. Every now and then there will be an assortment of unusual and exotic plant material from abroad.

59

Storing dried material

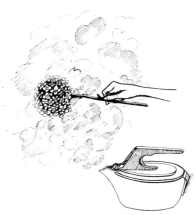

Refreshing tired and mis-shapen material

Dried items are best stored in cardboard boxes with tissue paper protecting the most fragile pieces. Always cover to protect from dust. Try not to overfill the boxes or crowd the plant material which, because of its fragility, breaks easily. Avoid completely enveloping a box with polythene for this holds in any possible residue of moisture and can ruin a boxful. If polythene is used always leave one end open. Newspaper is absorbent and is good as a packing material. A small bag of silica gel in each box will collect any lingering moisture; it may need reactivating from time to time. If you have a really dry place to keep the boxes you should have no difficulties. List the contents of each box on the outside to prevent frenzied rummaging when something is wanted in a hurry.

Tired-looking, misshapen, dried plants may be revitalized by being held in steam from a kettle. Some plants will only need a shake to re-shape them; others can be manipulated by hand. Be sure these are dry before they are stored away.

Drying with desiccants

Although the results from this method of drying are very fragile, the retention of colour and form are so exciting that all the trouble is worthwhile. Such arrangements do need the protection of a dome however, similar to the one in colour photograph 3. The Victorians used the dome to cover stuffed birds, shells, feathers and wool flowers. Sometimes old ones may be found in antique shops but modern versions are stocked by shops specializing in flower arranging equipment. These domes prevent desiccant-dried flowers from absorbing humidity from the atmosphere.

Silica gel

Physalis franchetii has been opened out to make larger shapes for this double arrangement. Also included are orange helichrysums, glycerined eucalyptus, *Thalictrum adiantifolium* and *Choisya ternata*

Desiccants remove the water content from the plant material by absorbing it. There are branded desiccants on the market which contain silica gel, and silica gel itself is sold in both granular and powder forms by chemists. The powder form is the best. It has the advantage of not being sticky or clogging together and of absorbing 50 percent of its own weight in water. After use it must be dried carefully by heating in an oven on a flat tray at a temperature of $121\,°C\,(250\,°F)$ for about 30 minutes. It will need a stir during this time. Special paper or some other means of measuring the water

61

content is often sold with silica gel powder. Sometimes the powder or crystals are coloured blue and change to a pinkish grey as they become saturated with moisture and need reactivating. Fresh silica gel acts fiercely, but it can be used over and over again, becoming gentler in its action as time goes on.

A bride's posy, or flowers for any occasion can be preserved in a desiccant, rearranged and perhaps kept under a dome as a memento. Silica gel is the quickest desiccant to use and may take as short a time as 24 hours for thin-petalled flat flowers such as violas.

Borax, alum, sand etc.

Alum and borax have the virtue of being very fine-grained and so do not mark the flower petals as a coarse silica gel does. They do, however, become sticky and may clog in the crevices between the petals. Sand has to be washed many times to ensure it is clean, and then dried before use. Sand is the slowest-acting desiccant and may take weeks in a warm place. Clean silver sand may be purchased from a garden centre, and is especially useful for foliage. Alum and borax take a week or more depending on the density of the flower and its water content. Washing powder can also be used as a desiccant. It will take longer to dry flowers in this than in any other medium excepting sand.

It is best to experiment with various desiccants as it is impossible to lay down hard and fast rules. Many people find a mixture of alum and silica gel or borax and silica gel very efficient. The branded desiccants are excellent and save a great deal of trouble. If you decide to use one of the proprietary brands the instructions will come with the desiccant.

Method of using silica gel

❊ Collect the plant material when it is quite dry and do not condition it. Then, with the silica gel and a suitably-sized box to hand, deal with it at once so that it has no chance to flag.

❊❊ If you are making up your own desiccant, add three tablespoons of non-iodized salt to each quart of silica gel. This helps with the colour retention. Plastic boxes with lids are satisfactory, so are coffee tins with plastic lids. A lid is not essential but it ensures that nothing gets spilt and stops the gel picking up any unforeseen dampness in the room. Cover the bottom of the box with 1cm ($\frac{1}{2}$in) of desiccant.

❊❊❊ Cut off the stems, leaving 1cm ($\frac{1}{2}$in) and wire the flowers at once, coiling up the wire so that it acts as a support for them in the gel. It is harder to wire efficiently when the flowers have been treated.

OPPOSITE Preserving with silica gel. Usually the flowers are best placed face upwards. Space them well and gently filter the desiccant round them. Keep shaking the box to make sure the powder gets into all the crevices and is evenly distributed.

Spikes such as delphiniums need a
support of either soft wood or wire

64

✻✻✻✻ Usually the flowers are best placed face upwards. Space them well and gently filter the desiccant around them. Keep shaking the box to make sure the powder is getting into all the crevices and is evenly distributed. Pour in enough desiccant to cover the flowers to a depth of 2·5cm (1 in). Spikes, e.g. delphiniums, need a support of either soft wood or wire. Put on the lid and leave in a warm place. Try not to over-dry the flowers or they darken in colour and become very brittle.

✻✻✻✻✻ About 24 hours later for the flat flowers, and perhaps two–three days for heavier blooms, remove the lid and pour off the desiccant gradually. Catch the flowers as they fall out. They should feel papery; if they feel soft they need further time in the powder. Clean off the granules with a soft paint brush. The flowers will have lost their sheen and it is possible to brush on a little oil or to protect them with a fixative manufactured specially for the purpose (see page 141).

Flowers treated in this way must be kept dry. A dome is the perfect place for an arrangement. A small quantity of desiccant can be concealed in the dome to collect lurking moisture; it will need to be examined from time to time and reactivated when necessary.

Flowers not in use must be packed carefully with tissue paper and stored in airtight tins. Desiccant-dried material must never come into contact with water and so it is not advisable to combine fresh foliage, which will need water, with flowers dried in desiccant.

Flowers to choose for desiccant drying

It is worthwhile trying to dry anything that takes your fancy. You could be lucky with the most unexpected plant. The spring flowers such as daffodil, tulip, narcissus and crocus are the hardest to preserve. These seem to re-absorb water quickly and collapse. Flowers that always respond well to the treatment for me include:
Aquilegia
Calendula
Centaurea cyanus (cornflower)
Dahlia
Delphinium
Delphinium consolida (larkspur)
Dianthus carophyllus (carnation)
Hydrangea
Narcissus (small)
Philadelphus (mock orange)
Rose (foliage and flowers)
Rudbeckia
Spray carnation
Viola wittrockiana (pansy)
Zinnia elegans

A grey-green lichen covered thorn from a Cornish hedgerow is secured on a pinholder in a grey, ironstone container. The single fresh 'Schoolgirl' rose is in a tube of water

Fungi

There are many species of fungi growing in Britain, the commonest of which is *Polystictus versicolor*, called the bracket fungus because of its shape. Often you will find it on tree stumps or the fallen limbs of trees. Dry the pieces in the oven at a temperature of $93\,°C$ ($200\,°F$); when they are quite hard they are preserved. They can have an unpleasant smell until ready.

Napkin rings

You will need:
18cm ($7\frac{1}{2}$in) of strong cardboard roll 3·8cm ($1\frac{1}{2}$in) in diameter
Textured wallpaper or similar strong material
1 metre (1 yard) of 2·5cm (1 in) wide velvet ribbon
2 metres (2 yards) of gold cord not wider than 3mm ($\frac{1}{8}$in)
Small dried flowers
Pearl stamens
Spirit glue
Gold paint

From the roll cut cleanly six lengths each measuring 3cm ($1\frac{1}{4}$in). Cover these with strips of the wallpaper, then rub the edges with fine sandpaper to make them as smooth as possible. Paint the inside carefully with gold paint. When quite dry cover with velvet ribbon, leaving space each side for the gold cord. Trim the ribbon if necessary. Stick on the cord and decorate with small dried flowers and leaves, gilding the leaves if you wish.

Crystallizing flowers

Method 1

Cover one tablespoonful of gum arabic crystals with four tablespoonfuls of rose water. Put this into a screw-topped jar and shake it from time to time. It will have become sticky and ready for use in three days. With a soft brush coat all of the flower with this mixture. Large flowers may be dismantled and reassembled later. Dredge the painted flower with caster sugar and dry fairly quickly in

The instructions for making these
festive napkin rings are on page 68
Maker: Vera Bishop
Photographer: John Vagg

a warm place, e.g. near a heater or in the airing cupboard. These flowers should be used at once or they fade, but store them in an airtight tin if absolutely necessary.

Method 2

Whip the white of an egg for a few seconds only. Choose a rose which is nearly fully out and dunk it in the egg white. Dredge thoroughly with caster sugar and dry as suggested above. This is great fun to do for a party.

Dried fruit peel

Orange, lemon, lime and grapefruit peel can be dried and used in swags, plaques and collages. It can be cut into petal or leaf shapes. Orange peel is the easiest for it can be taken off the fruit neatly quartered.

Cut the peel to whatever shape you want and remove some of the pith before drying it on a storage heater or between the oven and the grill (with only the oven on). The peel will not dry flat but is much livelier because of this. I usually trim it again when it is half dry and make some holes (if the skin is to be wired) with a darning needle or compass point. There is no need for the holes if the shapes are to be stuck into position.

Alternatively, dry the peel of grapefruit and oranges halved. Remove as much pith as possible. You will get a flattish circular shape and all that needs to be done is to give the round a centre and stem.

The natural colour of various types of fruit peel after drying blends exceedingly well with glycerined materials and the texture is pleasing.

Fruit skin will take oil-based paint, and I like painting it for this seems to enhance the texture.

Pomanders

A pomander makes a most acceptable present. These sweet-smelling devices were carried hanging from the wrist or held in the hand in Elizabethan times.

Choose a firm orange and divide it into four with tape. Stick cloves (approximately 50g/2oz) between the tape. When this has been done remove the tape and substitute velvet ribbon of the same width; if the ribbon is put on at the beginning there is a risk of soiling it with the oil from the fruit. Secure the velvet ribbon with pins and make a loop at the top for hanging the pomander. You can adorn the ribbon with pearls or other beads and give the finished pomander decorated ribbon tails. The clove-stuck orange is then dried near a boiler, room heater or in a warm airing cupboard. It is ready when it feels lightweight and hard.

Pot-pourri

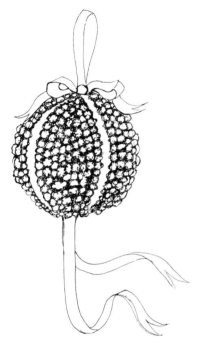

A beautiful bowl filled with musky scented *pot-pourri* is a delightful thing to have in the house. It is a reminder of the sweet scents of summer. It is also an attractive present.

The basis of most *pot-pourri* is rose petals, although almost any sweet smelling flowers, leaves and herbs can be added.

❋   The dry method of making *pot-pourri* seems to be the best. No salts or fixatives are included.

❋❋   Flower petals and herbs must be dried slowly at a low temperature. Too hot a temperature destroys the volatile oils.

❋❋❋   Dried and pounded orange and lemon peel and ground spices may be used. Mix well.

❋❋❋❋   Put into a bowl which has a well-fitting lid. Only remove the lid when the room is in use.

The following plants can be used for *pot-pourri*:

Bay leaves	Lemon thyme	Roses
Camomile	Lemon verbena	Stocks
Eau-de-cologne mint	Lime flowers	Tarragon
Lavender	Rosemary	

Making a pomander

4

Preserving with Glycerine

With this method of preservation the water content of leaves is replaced by glycerine. This makes the material very tough, pliable and sometimes glossy. The colour range is between pale cream and very dark brown. Many glycerined materials last for years; they can be used for a while and then carefully packed away again for another day. Leaves, bracts and some seed heads are suitable subjects for this treatment; flowers do not normally take glycerine. Glycerined material mixes well with a few fresh or silk flowers and you only need a small store of foliage to make versatile designs.

Glycerined foliage may be refreshed when necessary by washing in warm, mild detergent. Be sure to dry it properly afterwards.

OPPOSITE The three-tier hanging baskets contain small blocks of dry-foam taped in the centre. The glycerined plant material includes dark *Garrya elliptica* leaf sprays, ruscus, mahonia, *Choisya ternata*, Old Man's Beard and the pale cream flowers of *Molucella laevis* cut into separate whorls. Dried crocosmia, eryngium and phlomis, pine and alder cones complete the arrangement with leaf shapes cut from corn-cob husks. In the bottom basket a flower spray has been made by gluing honesty 'pennies' between the scales of the cones
Arranger: Daphne Vagg
Photographer: John Vagg

When to preserve

Deciduous foliage must be treated with the glycerine solution at the right stage of its development.

❋ It must be mature. Young spring foliage is too tender to absorb the heavy solution.

❋ The sap must still be rising. Towards autumn the leaf no longer takes up moisture: a protective cork-like barrier known as the abscission layer forms between the leaf and its stem, causing the leaf to wither and fall. When the abscission layer has started to form no glycerine can enter the leaf.

Mid-June until mid-August is the best time for most things, but there are certain exceptions which are listed on pages 78, 80.

Evergreen foliage will also make new growth in the spring, so wait until it has matured. Some evergreens are slow to take up the glycerine solution, especially during the winter months.

Method

The usual proportion is one part of glycerine to two parts of water.

Add two parts of boiling water to the glycerine in the measuring jug

✳   Put the glycerine into a measuring jug and add two parts of boiling water. Stir vigorously. Never heat glycerine – it is combustible.

✳✳   The foliage should have all damaged leaves, crossing branches and crowded stems removed. Break down very large branches into smaller pieces. Scrape the bark from the bottom 5cm (2 in) of the stem and cut upwards for about 2·5cm (1 in) to allow the glycerine and water to enter the stem more easily.

As long as the foliage is not flagging, there is no need to condition it before putting it into the solution, but tired material will not respond well to the glycerine.

✳✳✳   Choose a really stable vessel to hold the mixture and do not put in too much plant material. Air must be able to circulate. Put about 5–7cm (2–3in) of solution in the container; keep an eye on the level and top it up if necessary. Robust stems, e.g. branches of trees and woody shrubs, may be put into the glycerine mixture when it is quite hot. Warm water moves up the stem faster than cold.

Wait until the mixture is tepid for soft-stemmed plants. The mixture must be cold before any leaf is submerged.

If the pot is put in maximum light the plant material will be paler than if the process is carried out in the dark. You will get variations in colouring if you put some of the foliage in different lights.

✳✳✳✳   The process is complete when the leaves have all changed colour and feel silky. Usually the thinner the leaf the faster it responds to the glycerine.

✳✳✳✳✳   Material that has been left too long in the solution will get beads of glycerine on the surface of the leaves. This may be washed off with warm, weak detergent. Dry carefully.

Treating berries

Glycerine the berries of any material that carries them – often they take the solution quite well. Spray the berries with hair lacquer or a fixative to prevent them from falling off the branches.

Try cold anti-freeze, straight from the can, instead of glycerine. It can work fairly well as a substitute.

OPPOSITE Glycerined *Alchemilla mollis*, mahonia, beech, atriplex, spiraea, foxglove seed heads and wood roses from Trinidad are grouped around the figurine
Arranger: Alethia Chivers
Photographer: Peter Chivers

Treating thick, large leaves

Large leaves should be mopped frequently with the solution as well as having their stem ends in it. Some leaves, such as *Fatsia japonica*, may need a prop to hold the stem straight in the liquid. It is possible to submerge certain leaves completely, but a vessel large enough to hold them lying flat must be found. Some of these large leaves take quite a long time to change colour.

Pale cream material

One of the most prized plants for glycerining is the half-hardy annual *Molucella laevis* (Bells of Ireland). The bracts take the glycerine and turn the most wonderful pale cream. They also have a special scent. The flowers are small and insignificant and should be removed. The topmost bracts of molucella often fail to take up the glycerine because they are not fully developed. Try to catch this plant at the right moment when the top bracts are just open.

Other plants which are easy to come by and glycerine to a lovely cream colour are:
Aspidistra (a houseplant)
Choisya ternata (Mexican orange)
Danae racemosa
Fatshedera lizei (a houseplant)
Polygonatum odoratum (Solomon's seal)
Ruscus aculeatus
These plants can be dyed at the same time as they are glycerined. Mix the dye with water before combining it with the glycerine. Very pretty veining results.

Storage

A box, plenty of tissue paper and newspaper will keep the glycerined materials in good order. They must be kept in a dry place or they will go mouldy, but too hot a place will eventually dry them out. Do label the boxes if you have several – it saves so much time.

An antique alabaster urn holds a traditional collection of glycerined and dried material. *Grevillea robusta*, amaranthus, montbretia, eucalyptus, fatsia japonica, poppy seed heads and fir cones make up this formal arrangement
Arranger: Beryl Gray

Plant material suitable for glycerining

An asterisk * on the table overleaf marks the material obtainable from a florist, either sold by the stem or as a pot plant.

A dagger † beside a plant name means it can be found in the countryside.

Latin name	Common name	When to glycerine. Appearance after treatment	Time taken
Adiantum spp (hardy)	Maidenhair fern	Mature growth. Mid-brown. Reliable	2/3 weeks
†*Alchemilla mollis*	Lady's mantle	When in flower. Greenish-beige	2 weeks
*Aspidistra	—	Pale brown	3/4 months
Aquilegia vulgaris and others	Columbine	Seed heads – June	2 weeks
Buxus	Box	Any time as long as growth is mature. Soft tan	4 weeks or longer
Cercis siliquastrum	Judas tree	June. Rich cocoa brown	2/3 weeks
Choisya ternata	Mexican orange	Mature growth. Creamy	4 weeks or longer
Clematis spp	—	Seed heads of various varieties. 'Nellie Moser' is very good	2 weeks
†*Clematis vitalba*	Old man's beard	Treat when in flower	2 weeks
Cotoneaster	—	All varieties. Dark brown	4/5 weeks
*Danae racemosa	—	Arching sprays. Treat as soon as obtained. Pale brown	3/4 weeks
†*Digitalis*	Foxglove	Treat just before top flowers fade. Mid-brown	2 weeks
Eucalyptus	—	Greyish-purple	3 weeks
†*Fagus*	Beech	Must be mature. The colour varies according to light given during treatment	7–10 days
*Fatshedera	—	Any time. Best submerged. Cream	6 weeks or longer
*Fatsia japonica	—	Support and mop. Dark brown	Slow – 8 weeks
—	*Ferns	Treat when spores are showing. Submerge	2 weeks
*Ficus elasticus decora	Rubber plant	Submerge	2/3 weeks
Garrya elliptica	—	Spring, when tassels are at their best. Dark brown	3/4 weeks
*Grevillea robusta	—	Any time. No need to submerge. Dark brown	2/3 weeks
Hellebore	—	Leaves – especially 'Corsicus'. Mid-brown	3/4 weeks
†*Hosta*	Plantain lily	Pale brown. Submerge	3/4 weeks

Wall vases make good containers for dried arrangements. The cherub supports a shelf on which is a shallow tin containing dry foam. The traditional group includes *Molucella laevis*, *Lunaria annua* seed pods, *Choisya ternata*, fatshedera, *Alchemilla mollis* and seed heads of *Clematis* × 'Nellie Moser'. The flowers are made from araucaria leaves

Latin name	Common name	When to glycerine. Appearance after treatment	Time taken
Humulus lupulus	Hop	Treat flowers in autumn	2 weeks
Lunaria	Honesty	Treat when seed pods are green. Cream	2 weeks
Mahonia aquifolium	Oregon grape	Any time when growth is mature. Dark brown	2/3 weeks
M. bealii	—	Treat single leaves in different light. Various browns	2/3 weeks
Molucella laevis	Bells of Ireland	Treat when the top bracts are open. Creamy-white	2 weeks
Paeonia	—	Leaves and seed heads. Chestnut brown.	2/3 weeks
Pittosporum	—	Tobacco brown	2/3 weeks
Polygonatum odoratum	Solomon's seal	Treat in May. Cream	2/3 weeks
†*Quercus*	Oak	June/July. Golden brown. Acorns will stay on	2/3 weeks
Ribes	Flowering currant	Treat soon after flowers have faded. Rich brown	2 weeks
Rodgersia pinnata	—	Mid-summer	3 weeks
Rosa spp	Rose (including dog rose)	Trim chosen branches well. Mid-brown	2/3 weeks
Ruscus aculeatus	Butcher's broom	Deep cream	3/4 weeks
†*Sorbus aucuparia*	Mountain ash or rowan	Treat when in fruit in autumn. Spray fruit with fixative	3 weeks
Stephanandra flexuosa	—	Late summer	2/3 weeks
†*Thalictrum adiantifolium*	Meadow rue	When mature. Tobacco brown	2/3 weeks
†*Tilia*	Lime	Strip off the leaves and treat flowers	2 weeks

5

Skeletonizing, Bleaching & Using Dried Wood

Skeleton leaves

The Victorians loved skeletonized material, and they made the delicate pieces into 'phantom bouquets'. How attractive these must have looked, protected from dust under a dome. In skeletonizing, the entire epidermis of the leaf is removed, leaving only the 'bonework' of main ribs and tiny veins.

Skeletonized magnolia leaves can be bought from a florist or garden centre, usually in several different sizes. If you have a magnolia, camellia or holly it is worth while hunting around underneath the trees to see if nature has skeletonized some leaves for you, as it is a very time consuming and exacting occupation to do yourself. *Molucella laevis* bracts, hydrangea heads, physalis, *Nicandra physalodes* and lavatera calyces will also skeletonize.

Method

✻   Choose fresh, healthy leaves and pick them from the tree.

✻✻   Soak the leaves in rainwater, in a shady place, for about two months. The surface will then feel slippery and should be easy to remove (it may smell unpleasant).

✻✻✻   Rinse well and if the leaves are not white enough, put them into a mild solution of bleach for an hour.

✻✻✻✻   Rinse again and dry flat; press if necessary. The exception is the holly – these leaves have a natural curl.

Alternative methods

❋   Boil the leaves in a mixture of household soda and water for about an hour. Use a handful of soda to 1 litre (2 pints) of water. Or, boil the leaves in water into which half a packet of strong detergent has been emptied.

❋❋   Run cold water over a leaf to see if the green can be removed; if it cannot, boil longer.

❋❋❋   Rinse, bleach if necessary and dry.

Bleaching

Ready-bleached plant material can be found at garden centres and florists' shops. Cones, *Ruscus aculeatus* and ferns are the most often available, although barley, wheat, oats and many grasses look as if they have been whitened and groomed. This ivory-coloured material has a pleasant lightening effect in an arrangement and gives good contrast to the brown shades of glycerined leaves.

Bleaching at home is not difficult, provided you have a vessel long enough to take the whole length of a stem. You often also need some means of keeping the material submerged.

The usual proportion is half a bottle of household bleach to half a bucket of water. The cheaper the bleach, the longer the process takes. When the material is pale enough, rinse it well before drying it, in the sun if possible.

A few minutes in bleach improves the appearance of many plants as long as they are not fragile. Very delicate material may disintegrate in time but the seed heads of the crown imperial, camassia, the tougher alliums, *Lavatera trimestris* (do not bleach the dark brown 'buttons'), hogweed and many lilies will benefit from being washed in bleach.

Dried wood

OPPOSITE This 'ribcage' of ivy once grew round a tree trunk; stripped of its bark it is as white as bone. It has been set into a plaster base which holds it firmly. The glycerined aralia leaf hides the plaster and also makes a background for three silk poppies

Many people love dried wood in flower arrangements, others shun it: they do not want it in their homes and feel it is incongruous to have a piece of unfashioned tree as a decoration. Perhaps it is too reminiscent of wet undergrowth and creepy-crawlies. But the effect need not be rugged and rural. Stripped ivy can have the colour and

texture of ivory, and the smoother and more polished the wood, the greater the degree of sophistication it acquires. I once used to reject wood but I have learned to appreciate it for it has much in its favour.

One of the most important attributes of dried wood is that it helps to make a few flowers go such a long way. For those limited to the odd bunch it is a godsend. Wood is also natural plant material and every kind of tree or shrub is completely individual in its graining, growth habit and colour. One thing is certain: every piece of dried wood is unique, for no two bits are ever alike.

It is fun to search for wood on beaches, near lakes and streams, in old quarries, under hedges and in woods. Sometimes pieces can be bought already cleaned from flower club stalls and garden centres which specialize in flower-arranging equipment.

More often than not a 'find' will need some alteration; perhaps a small crossing branch may spoil the line and would be better sawn off; or the addition of another branch is necessary to increase the height. Most scars can be camouflaged by sanding or the use of plastic wood to cover the wound, which later may be carefully coloured to match the rest.

Fresh, live wood must be stripped of its bark at once. Not only does it come off easily if done immediately, but the colour underneath is clean and bright. This is especially important with ivy and tortuoso willow which are both nearly white and require no further treatment.

Preparing wood

Unless you are fortunate enough to find wood that has been washed clean by the sea, loch or stream, the usual practice is to:

❋　　Wash it thoroughly. When it is dry, get rid of all the loose bits – a pointed knife will do the job. Never waste time on rotten wood.

❋❋　　Brush with a wire brush unless the wood is grey in colour. Grey wood needs to be treated with care in order to preserve this attractive finish which is only on the surface. Also omit the brushing if the wood has a natural polish.

❋❋❋　　It is a pity to varnish or wax naturally grey wood, but less pleasing surfaces may be sanded. The prepared wood can be varnished, though this tends to look a little artificial. It can be rubbed with linseed oil, wood stain or shoe polish. Chalk will sometimes succeed in giving a silvery colour.

❋❋❋❋　　Wood can be bleached by being immersed in a bucket of water containing half a bottle of bleach. Make sure the whole of the wood is covered by the mixture; weigh it down if necessary or use an old bath or bowl that will be big enough to take the whole piece. Bleach gives a slightly yellow tinge to wood; a half block of salt in a bucket of water gives a greyer effect. Always rinse well and dry in the sun.

OPPOSITE Clever mechanics make it possible to use fresh plant material in all the openings of this versatile piece of driftwood. The waxy anthuriums with their smooth edges contrast well with the narrow lanceolate leaves of *Hellebore foetidus*
Arranger: Susan Julian

Mechanics for dried wood

Pinholders

Lightweight pieces of wood fix on to a pinholder quite satisfactorily. It may be necessary to split the ends of the wood to allow the pins to penetrate properly. Slightly larger pieces of wood can have holes drilled into their ends and a short length of soft wood may be inserted into each hole and glued. The softer wood will be more easily impaled. Cane, wisteria and lonicera pieces will fix on to a pinholder successfully.

Foam

Only lightweight bits of wood should be put into foam. A 'tripod' of wire will prevent too big a hole being made in the foam.

Clamps

There are clamps available in various sizes specially made to hold wood firmly. There are different patterns; some have a pinholder on their underside which fits on to a second pinholder. Very heavy clamps for large pieces of wood are available.

This large round of elm with its hollow centre would make a good permanent frame for flowers in a large, modern building. Two fresh 'Enchantment' lilies are in a pinholder
Arranger: Mary Patterson

Mechanics for dried wood:
a Lightweight pieces on a pinholder
b and c Clamps

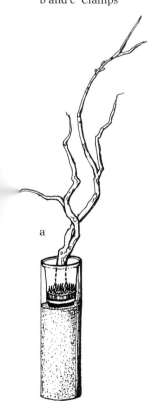

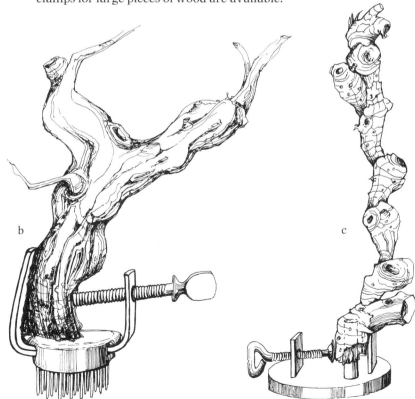

a

b

c

OPPOSITE Here is a striking use for an enormous piece of dried wood. Remove the bromeliads from their pots and wrap the root balls in sphagnum moss (obtainable from a florist), then tie them into a crevice in the wood with plastic-covered wire. Spray the moss frequently and keep the central well of the plants filled with water. The wood belongs to Catherine Green and Mollie Howgate assembled the plants

Screws

One piece of wood can be anchored permanently to another which acts as a base. This is done by drilling a hole through the base from underneath. Then a screw is inserted on to which the dried wood is screwed, thus attaching it to the base.

False legs

These can be nailed or screwed on to a heavy piece of wood so that it will stand at the required angle. Holes the same diameter as lengths of dowelling rod can be drilled in heavy wood. The dowelling may be slightly sharpened at one end and hammered into the holes. Use glue for extra security.

Plaster

Various plasters are useful for holding branches for landscape designs and for some Christmas decorations. The end of the wood is embedded in enough plaster to hold it upright. Use a piece of thick cardboard cut to the desired shape as a base for the plaster. When the plaster has dried it can be painted and sprayed.

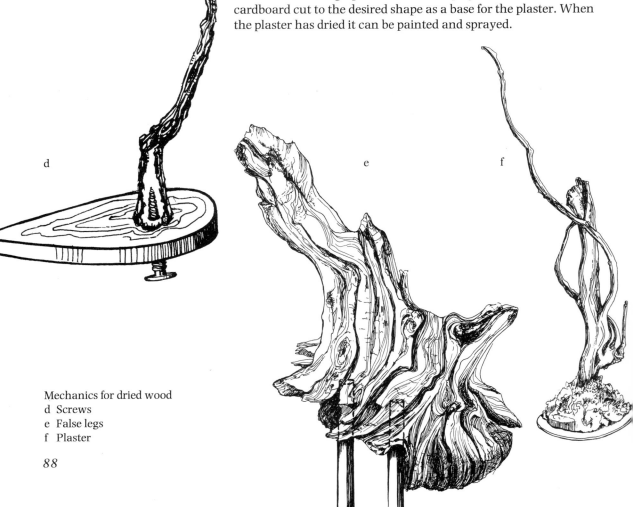

d

e

f

Mechanics for dried wood
d Screws
e False legs
f Plaster

6

Wiring, Containers & Mechanics

Wiring helichrysums

OPPOSITE The bold, modern, brownish container hides a pinholder. The large area of the top opening is diminished by the wood. *Salix glandulosa* 'Setsuka' gives height and movement and the yellow helichrysums are bunched to give an impression of large flowers. One glycerined *Mahonia bealei* leaf hides the wired stem of the tallest flowers and adds a little shiny texture

Wiring

Unless you know a little about wiring techniques it is difficult to make the most of your glycerined and dried plant material so that it shows to advantage and stays firmly in position.

Wires for flowers are made in different gauges and lengths, varying between 32 gauge and 18 gauge; the thicker the wire the lower the gauge. A wire of 18 gauge is quite strong and too thick to use for any purpose other than making a stem for a large flower or for wiring heavy fruit on to a garland. Wires thicker than 24 gauge are usually sold already cut into stem lengths between 18cm (7in) and 35·5cm (14in), sometimes called stub wires. The thinner bundles of cut wire are known as rose wires. Reel wire (a spool of wire) comes in various gauges.

You need some sort of tape, made specially for the purpose, for covering the wire stems. Tapes have a slightly tacky surface that adheres to the wire easily, helped by the heat of the hand. They are sold in tones of green, brown and white. Brown is best for blending with dried and glycerined things; white is useful for the small pink and white acrocliniums and helipterums and for Christmas decorations. I use green only when the wired material is to be mixed with fresh foliage.

It is better to wire helichrysums with 22 gauge or 24 gauge stub wire before hanging them up to dry. A wire is simply pushed through the centre of the flower: it will go into the moist, newly picked flower easily. The natural dampness corrodes the wire and the flower together. If you wish to be absolutely certain that the false stem will be safe, make a hook at the top of the wire, though this is not necessary unless you are wiring a flower that is already dry.

Acrocliniums, rhodanthe and helipterums can be wired in the same way but need a finer wire. Xeranthemums can retain their

Method for wiring any flower with a prominent seed case, e.g. carnation

strong little woody stems. If small flowers have to be wired after they have dried it is better not to force the wire through the flower's centre but to use the inch or so of stem remaining under the calyx. If you are grouping small flowers in garlands or swags they will need a wire stem, but for collage they do not need to be wired.

Any flower with a prominent seed case (e.g. carnations) to be dried in a desiccant must have one or two wires put through the seed case before it is placed in the drying medium. When the flower is to be arranged the wires are curved downwards to form a stem, and one leg of wire is twisted round the other a few times. The excess wire is cut off, thus preventing everything becoming heavy and bulky, and spoiling the professional look.

The hair-pin method of wiring is the most satisfactory whenever it is possible. It ensures that the wire will not slip out from the object it is attached to; the leaf or flower is trapped between the two legs of the hair-pin. For this method to be effective there must be a portion of stem left on the plant material. If a leaf has lost all of its stalk (petiole) cut each side of the main rib to make a new projection. After the wire stem has been taped firmly the result is remarkably reliable although all wired pieces need careful handling and renovation from time to time.

One of the great advantages of using wired plant material is that the stems can be curved to any angle.

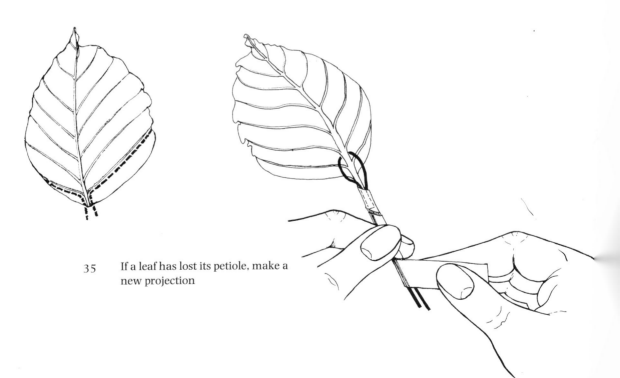

35   If a leaf has lost its petiole, make a new projection

Wiring leaves

❊   Take a 26 gauge wire and with the back of the leaf facing you make a stitch across the main rib about 2·5–5cm (1–2in) from the base. Hair-pin the wire and wind one of the legs around the leaf stem and the second leg of wire.

The stitch method of wiring a leaf

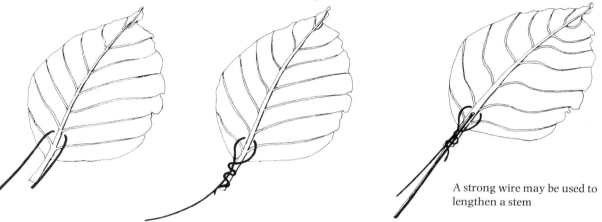

A strong wire may be used to lengthen a stem

If you wish to lengthen the stem, add a stronger stub wire before twisting the leg. Leaves can be grouped to form a spray.

❊   A stronger wire may be taped to the back of a larger leaf. Then make a hair-pin from a fine wire and bind it round the petiole, strong wire and leg.

For leaves such as aralia a piece of flat wood, with a sharpened end, may be used instead of the strong wire.

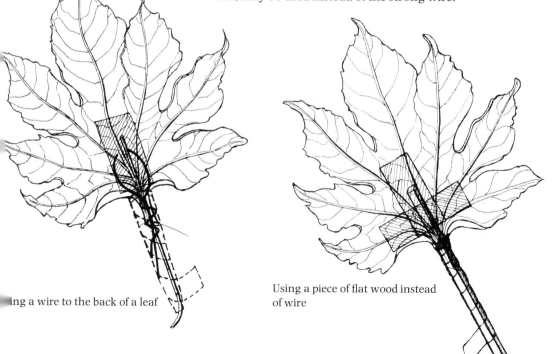

ing a wire to the back of a leaf

Using a piece of flat wood instead of wire

93

✳   A fine wire may simply be hair-pinned and twisted round the petiole, leaving the loop (so that the main stem is not squeezed) at the top and back of the leaf.

Pressed bracken

A length of reel wire of approximately 28 gauge or 30 gauge, zigzagged up the stem of pressed bracken between the fronds, makes it easy to curve the whole stem and so avoid the flat stiffness that results from pressing.

Fixing a fine wire

Wiring pressed bracken

Cones

Cones can be wired with two wires (choose a gauge to suit the weight of the cone) which are twisted together at the bottom of the cone.

Beech mast

A hair-pin of wire is put round the centre and twisted below (see page 58).

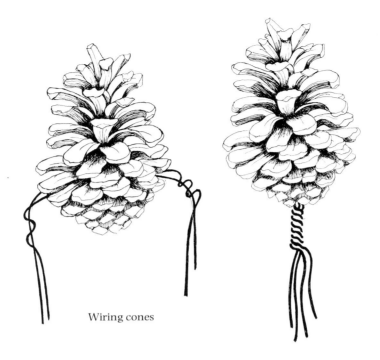

Wiring cones

Nuts, fruit stones

These should be held in a vice while a small hole is drilled through the shell. It is then simple to thread a wire through the hole and twist it to make a stem.

Gourds

Gourds are hollow when they are dry. Make two holes near together if you wish to wire them, or one hole for a wooden stick. This must then be glued. A glue gun is a useful possession.

Sweet chestnuts, horse chestnuts, acorns and plane tree fruits

If necessary make small holes through the chestnut cases with a compass point. Glue the conkers into the cases and wire through the holes. Plane tree fruits may be quite firmly fixed on their own stems, but if necessary make two holes at the base of each fruit and wire. Cupless acorns will need a small hole through the base of the fruit for a wire. Glue an acorn into its cup and wire through holes made in the cup.

An S-shaped garland to decorate the table. The basis is a wire S (made from coathanger wire) bound with florists' stem-binding tape. Each piece of dried and glycerined material is wired separately and twisted firmly round the base wire. The colouring ranges from the very dark brown of glycerined mahonia and garrya leaves to the creamy 'leaves' cut from corn-cob husks. *Choisya*

ternata leaves provide a dull khaki colour and the heads of phlomis have retained a good grey-cream. Beech nut cases, various cones and peach stones (drilled with a tiny hole for wiring) provide contrasting textures. Bright tan candles and napkins complement the pale blue cloth.
Arranger: Daphne Vagg
Photographer: John Vagg

OPPOSITE The container used for this arrangement is a modern one and it holds a large pinholder. The yucca gives the design movement and is a good foil for the *Eryngium giganteum* flowers which have been given stout false stems
Arranger: Sheila Addinall

False stems of plant material

It is disheartening and exasperating for a beginner when the plant material refuses to stay put; annoying enough sometimes to make one despair of ever getting anything right! The mechanics of flower arranging may be basic but this does not mean that they are always simple. Good mechanics are more important than any other single factor. With experience you will learn how a stem will behave in your chosen mechanics, and in time you will be able to assess the weight of a flower head; but for a beginner it can be bewildering and frustrating.

Flower arrangers should never throw anything away, even though overflowing boxes are one of the minor disadvantages of the occupation. Make a collection of strong hollow stems to use as false stems or pinholder supports for weak or wired subjects. Hogweed, cow parsley, phlox and pampas grass are just some of the plants with conveniently supportive stems for this purpose. A lightweight dried flower with a taped wire stem will cause little trouble when it is put into dry foam or sand, but if it has to be impaled on a pinholder the wire end may easily be too fine to secure. If the end is pushed into a hollow stem which is fixed on to the pinholder the result is a rock-like firmness. A false stem of the right strength and calibre must be chosen to suit each flower.

Heavy heads such as artichokes, some hand-made flowers and unusual foreign seed pods must have a thick wire or wood support before being placed in a sturdy, hollow stem.

Heavy-headed pieces or artificial Christmas sprays may swing around in either wet or dry foam, so try giving them a tripod foot (see illustration). Remember that taped stems of wire and plastic will be more stable than untaped ones. Be sure to choose a wire of the correct gauge for a particular task: too thick a wire will give a clumsy result, and too thin a wire will fail to carry the load. Wiring and taping well is a knack and practice makes perfect.

Containers

There are innumerable containers on the market; many are cheap plastic copies of classical shapes, and these are often quite pleasing except for their texture and weight. Before you buy one of these look to see if there is a hollow underneath the base that could be filled with plaster to give it stability. Also make sure that the cup is large enough to take a sensible amount of foam. Some are very tiny. Cheap containers may be made to look twenty times more valuable if

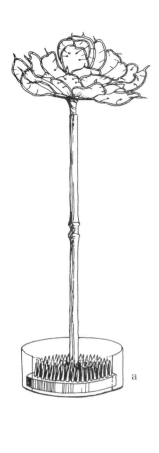

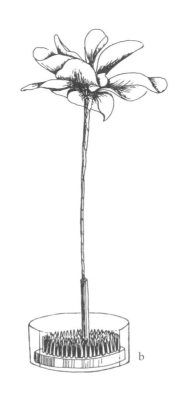

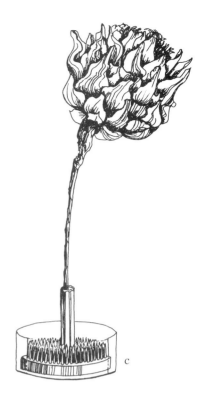

a Lightweight flower with false stem

b Made-up wired double flower with wire stem and false stem at the bottom

c Heavy artichokes wired with a strong wire and supported in a stout false stem

d Give artificial or very heavy material a tripod foot

OPPOSITE An unusual design of
interesting lines and rounds. The
container is constructed from a
thick piece of hogweed stem and
maximum use is made of the
enclosed space. The hogweed stem
holds a tin in which there is a
pinholder.
Arranger: Beryl Grisdale

Flowers and plants arranged on
two levels are always arresting.
The white wire cage has pot plants
in it but would look attractive used
as a container for a dried design
Arranger: Mollie Howgate

OPPOSITE A small painted basket holds a simple collection of pale helipterums, dryas seed heads, grasses and anaphalis

they are painted with matt paint, and before the first coat is dry they can be brushed over in places with a slightly darker colour. Small tins of paint for model makers are easily obtainable. Olive green, antique bronze, greys, tobacco browns and soft sludgy colours give the most satisfactory effect. If you want a glaze, a gloss paint, polyurethane or an artist's clear varnish can be used.

The most expensive containers, often figurines, are made from substances that resemble marble or soapstone, or they are pottery. They are usually a yellowish-white or pale green in colour. I think these are given more individuality if they are carefully subdued, the recessed parts darkened, and the rather blatant shine reduced. Shoe polish works wonders, or matt paint on cotton wool, judiciously and thinly smeared over the figurine. This will give the container an antique look.

Somehow the flower arranger must compensate for the lack of life in the preserved material by highlighting the qualities of texture, form and line characteristic of the material. The right container is of the utmost importance; it should not dominate but it plays a vital part in the presentation.

Styles

✻ In the small traditional arrangements of grasses and *immortelles*, with their sugared-almond colours, delicate china, even patterned, is pretty. The normally eschewed white vase and lightweight painted baskets are delightful too. Natural cane baskets do not usually provide enough contrast with the brown tones and shades that result from drying and glycerining.

✻ Traditional mass arrangements of dried and glycerined pieces are often enhanced by a glazed pot or a rich looking container.

✻ A modern arrangement needs a contemporary vase of good design. There are some wonderful ones on the market and some horrors which are much too fussy. A desirable modern container depends on clean lines and good proportions. It will have an interesting texture and colour, and not rely on extraneous surface decoration. The trend is for two openings or two (sometimes more) positions for flowers. This enlarges the design by giving the eye further to travel.

If a modern container is too expensive try making one or two for yourself.

Shallow lead container

You will need a sheet of lead, which can usually be obtained from a plumber. Strong scissors, a small wooden mallet or padded hammer are also necessary.

Shallow lead container

A Victorian footbath makes an ideal holder for a *pot-et-fleur*. This is an assortment of growing plants either in compost or grouped in their individual pots in the container. Cut flowers may be added if you wish
Arranger: Joyce Monks

Cut a piece of paper to the shape you require for the base of your container. Cut the lead to this pattern, leaving a margin of at least 4cm (1½in). Knock up the sides with the mallet, or hammer against a block of wood. Bevel the edges with a file.

Shallow tin containers

Any rectangular shallow tin can be made into a container and raised on small feet. Stick four half cotton reels or small identical blocks of wood under the tin before covering it with the kind of modelling clay that is sold wrapped in foil in art shops. This does not need firing. Give the clay surface a texture: I have used a shell, an ammonite and a vegetable grater to advantage at different times. Leave the container to dry thoroughly and then paint it inside and out. Waterproofing may be done with polyurethane varnish.

Container with double top openings

This is a home-made version of a Japanese container. It is especially useful for putting fresh plant material with dried. One opening can have crumpled wire netting (only a small piece is needed) or dry foam, and the other water or wet foam.

The container is made from two tins, one 5cm (2in) deep with a diameter of 6·5cm (2½in) and the other 11·5cm (4½in), diameter 9cm (3½in). The two tubes have a diameter of 2·5cm (1in) and are 10cm (4in) long.

Shallow tin container

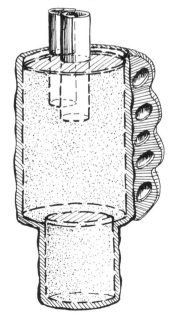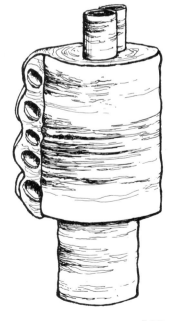

Containers with double top openings

Container with two openings

A container may be made quickly
from a milk bottle

Both tins are first weighted with clean sand, and bonded to each other with a strong cardboard disc sealing in the sand in the bottom tin. The open end of the larger tin is at the top. Another circle of card forms the top of the larger tin and has two circles cut in it of the exact diameter of the tubes. The tubes are pushed through the card and into the sand which holds them firmly. Glue the tubes to the card before putting on the rolled out modelling clay. The projection, which adds a great deal to the overall appeal of the container, is clay. Texture the clay and leave to dry, and paint it as you wish.

Container with two openings

Two 5cm (2in) and one 11·5cm (4½in) high tins with a diameter of 9cm (3½in) are required.

Weight one of the 5cm (2in) tins with sand or plaster. When the plaster is dry, seal, cover and glue on strong card cut to fit the tin.

Stick the second 5cm (2in) tin containing a 5cm (2in) pinholder, with a section of one side cut away, on top of the first.

Fill the larger tin two-thirds full of sand or plaster and glue it on top of the second tin.

When quite set, cover the tins with a modelling clay to give either a completely smooth surface, or a textured one marked in some way, e.g. with criss-cross lines or a grater.

When the clay is dry, paint the container. Neutral colours are the most versatile, and matt or gloss paint may be used.

The top opening takes a 6·5cm (2½in) pinholder.

Quick containers

A quick but effective container can be made from a milk bottle filled with sand for dried material, or water for fresh, with a twist of 5cm (2in) mesh chicken wire wedged in the neck. The bottle may be camouflaged with a slip-over cover made out of a bamboo table mat or a cylindrical cardboard tube around which some textured material has been glued.

Other quick containers may be created out of tubular tins used for household cleaners and again covered with material or string. These will need to be weighted with sand up to the height where a small yoghurt or cream carton (painted the same colour as the container's surface) is fitted in. Remember that the small cartons will only hold a 4cm (1½in) pinholder. Crumpled chicken wire may be placed on top of the pinholder. These containers are approximately 18cm (7in) tall, and an acceptable size for the average modern home.
An arrangement of the usual proportions will stand about 46cm (18in) high.

Quick containers made from tubular tins

Using a base

❉ A base acts in the same way as a frame: it presents the design. It also protects the surface of furniture.

❉ In interpretative work the base is an integral part of the design, and is essential when accessories and more than one placement are used, for it unites these.

❉ A base must exactly suit the style of the design, as do the scroll base on page 108, and the wood base on page 100.

❉ In the home a base is not always desirable, especially when the flower arrangement happily and naturally adorns the setting. (See colour plate 40).

❉ If a container is used that is large at the bottom, a further base is unnecessary. Also, some modern arrangements do not need a base – they are complete without.

Mechanics

Dry mechanics

Preserved plant material needs 'dry' mechanics, but as it is water which provides the necessary bottom weight that helps to ensure the stability of a fresh design, some substitute for it must be found.

❉ A lead pinholder 7·5cm (3in) in diameter will on its own give a firm anchor for an arrangement in a shallow dish or bowl.

❉ A tall container can be given bottom weight if it is filled up to pinholder level with clean sand.

❉ A deep container for a traditional mass arrangement may also be weighted with sand. The addition of 5cm (2in) chicken wire, crumpled, gives excellent additional support.

❉ Dry foam is pleasant to use and allows the lovely loose downward movement that is so desirable in a raised arrangement. It does, however, need to be secured, either in a heavy container with tape or a cap of 2·5cm (1in) or 5cm (2in) chicken wire, or in a container made heavy at the base so that it does not overbalance. Many inexpensive stemmed containers have a hollow under the foot that can be filled with plaster of some kind. This will give good bottom weight.

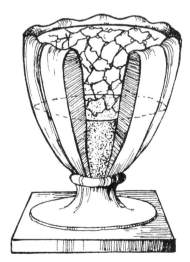

Sand and chicken wire used to give support in a deep container

A block of foam fixed in a container with tape

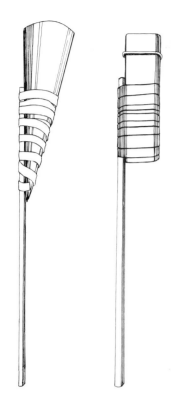

Cones and tubes

A Chinese red lacquer container provides a pleasing foil for gold-sprayed dried plant material with interesting forms. Included are leaves, seed heads or branches from the following plants: *Afzelia quanzensio*, *Plumeria rubra* (frangipani), *Proboscidea louisianica*, *Bougainvillea glabra*, *Strelitzia reginae* and *Nelumbo nucifera* (lotus)
Arranger: Joyce Monks

Wet mechanics

It is obvious that fresh plant material must have water, and failure to supply it is one of the reasons for disqualification in a competition. It is after all only common sense: without water a flower will not live its normal life span. Succulents and cacti, however, are not so affected.

In many of the arrangements photographed there are a few fresh flowers along with the dried or glycerined pieces. These are all in wet mechanics of some kind. Sometimes the stems of the preserved material are in the same mechanics and so sharing the water, in which case the ends of the preserved plant material are protected by florists' tape or wax. If the fresh flowers are in wet mechanics of their own they are in tubes.

Cones and tubes

These vary in size. Their purpose is to provide water for:

❈ Short stems in a mass arrangement that cannot reach the mechanics.

❈ Flowers or foliage in modern and abstract designs where there is no visible container.

❈ Fresh flowers or foliage mixed with preserved.

There are water-retaining foam holders made of lead; unlike a pinholder they will only have a few long spikes. They hold the foam firmly and give valuable base weight.

There is a plastic version of the holder called a 'frog'. Frogs are cheap and lightweight, but they do stop the foam moving in small arrangements.

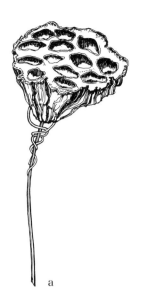

a

a Lotus seed head (*Nelumbo lutea*)
b A strip-wood stick or thin cane
may be glued to the back of pods,
cones and spathes. Left:
Aspidosperma verbascifolium
(elephant's ears); right: *Delonix
regia* (flamboyant pod)

Tape

There is a specially manufactured adhesive tape which may be
secured across the plastic foam, with the ends firmly stuck to the
container. It will stop the foam moving but of course gives no
weight.

Imported plant material

I had a great desire to name correctly all the imported plant material
which is so popular today. Unfortunately these pods and spathes are
hardly ever sold under their botanical name, which is a pity, as the
Latin name so ably describes the plant. They are called by common
or 'pet' names and identification is very difficult.

These additions to the stores of the flower arranger come from all
over the world, though mainly from tropical and sub-tropical
regions, South and East Africa, central America, South America and
Australia.

A large proportion of the imported materials are seed pods which
have the bold shapes lacking amongst preserved plant material in
Britain. The pods are often whole, containing seeds, though the open
and empty ones expose intriguing markings and intricate linings.
The lotus seed heads are familiar to most people as are the many
types of protea flower which may be purchased fresh and slowly
dried for future use.

The pods, cones and spathes of varying size are frequently heavy
and difficult to support. Either a strip wood stick or a thin cane
(6mm × 6mm; $\frac{1}{4}$in × $\frac{1}{4}$in) can be glued to the back of these. A glue
gun does the job most efficiently. Another way is to drill a small hole
in the base of a thick pod and insert a sharpened stick, plus a touch of
glue. Less weighty material can be wired with strong wire and then
taped in the usual way.

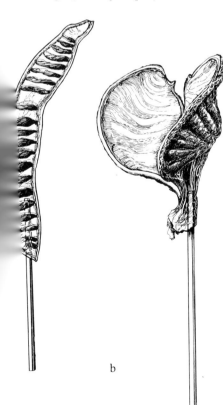

b

OPPOSITE A carved African head at
home among mathari lilies,
spathes, doum palm, raffia palm
cones and baskets. The group is of
warm browns and creams
Arranger: Dorothy Hudson

7

Made-up Flowers, Silk Flowers & Collage

Made-up flowers

Made-up flowers concocted from natural plant material have become a popular addition to the dried flower arrangement. Nature does not provide a good, dried, eye-holding form in Britain. The hydrangea heads, the large alliums and leek seed heads are the biggest round shapes available, and of these the hydrangea is the most solid, though it is far from being clear cut. The brightest are opened physalis, but these are small and the natural growth habit does not lend itself to forming a centre of interest unless each orange lantern is treated as a separate flower. From other countries come the lotus seed heads, the mathari lilies, wood roses and many fascinating seed pods of considerable size.

Made-up flowers fulfil the need for points of interest in a design. They give contrast and dominance and provide areas upon which the eye may rest. Definite, striking and clean shapes should be aimed at when making flowers: if they are too elaborate the whole idea is vitiated. Fussy flowers only add to the confusion of the dried mass arrangement which can so easily become a tangle. The modern design also needs bold shapes. Any made-up flowers may be painted or sprayed. These contrived flowers have a place not only in containers, but also in plaques, collages and three-dimensional pictures. In the photograph on page 113 the contrast of form from hand-made flowers is remarkable.

Made-up flowers can be divided into three groups: those that have a cardboard support, those that have a centre to which the stem wire is attached, and flowers made up entirely of wired petals. I have found that it strengthens the card used in the first group if a circle of hessian or similar material is glued to the top of the card. This prevents the card from tearing when the wires are pulled taut. A four-holed button of suitable size can be substituted for the card.

OPPOSITE This dreamy design has the title 'The Haunted Ballroom'. The preserved material was sprayed with a pale mauve poster paint and then oversprayed with a greyish-pink car spray
Arranger: Winifred Simpson
Photographer: James A. Fenemore

Single made-up flowers need a good centre. They may be made on a base and the centre simply superimposed after the petals have been glued. *Lavetera rosea* produces attractive, flat, round, brown centres.

There are several examples of made-up flowers in the illustrations and an explanation of each is given in the caption. There are so many possibilities, but the final choice depends on the material available and the taste of the maker.

Double flowers with a card base

❀ Rounds of thin card 4cm (1½in) in diameter will make a paeony-like flower from honesty pennies. Vary the size of the flowers a little so they are not too uniform.

❀❀ Glue similar-sized circles of hessian to the upper side of the card.

❀❀❀ Make four small holes in the covered card and thread two rose wires through the holes. Bind these wires tightly to an 18 or 20 gauge stem wire. Cover the bound part with a little cotton wool and tape the entire stem neatly.

❀❀❀❀ With a spirit glue, stick the 'petals' around the outer edge of the card and continue overlapping the petals until the card is covered. As you near the centre make the 'petals' come towards you to give the flower a heart. Cover the back of the card with 'petals' or paint it.

Wired double flowers

❀ Select leaves with a slight variation in size and wire each leaf carefully using the stitch method.

❀❀ Group three or five of the smallest leaves to form a centre and wire them to a stout stem wire.

❀❀❀ Continue to add leaves, gradually using larger ones, until the flower is of the size required. Cut away excess wire as you go.

❀❀❀❀ Neaten and tape as before.

Single flowers with seed head centres

Sometimes it is possible to use the seed head still on its natural stem. Make certain the stem is strong enough.

OPPOSITE Flowers made from wood shavings. First remove the centre of a fir cone and give it a strong wire stem. Next glue together wood shavings 3·8cm (1½in) wide and cut them into petal shapes. Cut five or six slightly smaller petals and glue them into the cone, curving them inwards. The larger petals are then added and curved away from the centre. The stem wire can be put into a hollow stalk *Wood flowers and arrangement: Elaine Fenwick*

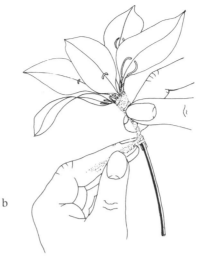

a Single made-up flower with a
lotus seed head centre
b Covering the wires with cotton
wool
c Taping

Single flower with small lotus seed head centre

✻   Wire the lotus seed head, giving it a stem.

✻✻   Surround the centre with suitable wired 'petals'; eliminate
excess wire as soon as the 'petals' are firm.

✻✻✻   Neaten with cotton wool and tape.

Single flowers with card base

Instead of filling the middle of the card with 'petals' leave room for a
plant material centre to be glued to the card.

'Petals'

Double flower

Artichoke bracts
Beech, glycerined
Eucalyptus, glycerined
Lunaria pennies
Maize sheaths
Skeletonized magnolia
Wood shavings

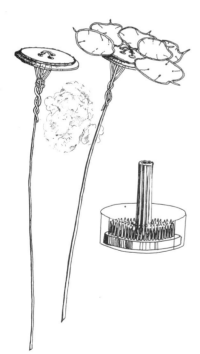

Single flower on a card base. Leave
room for a superimposed centre

Single flower

Araucaria araucana (Monkey puzzle)
Crown Imperial seed cases
Dried citrus fruit skins
Iris foetidissima (empty seed pods)
Lilies (various seed cases)
Wood shavings

Flower centres

Alliums (small)
Beech mast
Cones
Dipsacus (Fuller's teasle)
Eryngium spp
Lagurus ovatus (Harestail grass)
Lavatera rosea (the cap from the seed case)
Lotus seed heads (small)
Papaver somniferum
Papaver orientale

Silk flowers

In recent years there has been a marked improvement in the quality and realism of silk flowers and foliage. The best are made of polyester and are not cheap to buy, so they deserve to be looked after carefully when not in use. Cleverly mixed with natural plant material, it is sometimes difficult to decide whether they are real or silk. The large poppies and roses and trails of ivy are some of the most attractive.

Silk flowers are anathema to many people but they have their place in the overheated hairdressing salon, shop window displays and in the home when time is short.

The stems of silk flowers are their weakest point. A false hollow stem of natural plant material will help camouflage their ugly stiffness. Even simply taping stems will improve them, but they must be shortened or lengthened according to the needs of the design and a new wire stem will prove much more pliable.

If the foliage attached to the flowers is not sufficiently convincing try adding better silk foliage, e.g. ferns, ivies and philodendron, to help cover the stems. Glycerined foliage is ideal.

Collage

Our word collage comes from the French word *coller*, meaning to paste or glue. There is great scope here for the flower arranger to make wall hangings of various kinds, either framed, as in the illustration on the back cover, or not. The materials used are all glued to the background. They should not be glazed.

In a pressed picture all depth is illusory, but the collage has a third dimension. This gives a greater range for the enjoyment of texture, colour and shape. All sorts of styles are possible, from the traditional to the abstract, and on the whole the medium lends itself to a bold modern approach similar to that used in line arrangements. There is plenty of room for interpretation and self-expression.

Contemporary interiors often have large areas of bare wall where a collage will hang very happily. We live in times when people love to change the decor frequently: collages are not always permanent masterpieces and can be changed without great expense.

The number of materials available for use is limitless, but flower arrangers should aim at allowing the plant forms to predominate.

Materials

Gathering together materials for a collage is especially fascinating to a flower arranger. Single dried leaves and flowers, broken pieces from seed pods and small bits of wood can be hoarded, and often come in handy.

Natural materials

Bark
Bones (small)
Dried fruit peel
Dried grasses, leaves and flowers
Dried wood
Feathers
Fossils
Fruit stones
Gravel
Nut shells
Pebbles
Seaweed
Sea shells
Seeds and seed pods
Sponge

Sweet pea tendrils make the arms and anaphalis the faces of these little dancers. Other plant materials are quaking grass and roses dried in desiccant
Arranger: Freda Hart
Photographer: Jeremy Hall

Man-made materials

Cord
Fabric
Lace
Pearls and beads
Sequins
String

The surface texture of fabrics can be altered by scraping or wrinkling.

Colour

You can add colour to your collage by using aerosol sprays – car sprays are particularly effective. Try also bleaching, dyeing and painting. Oil paint has a less drying effect than water paint, which may need a polyurethane finish.

Adhesives

There are so many gums, glues and pastes that it is not easy to know which to choose for a particular job.

Rubber adhesives

These are good for pressed flower pictures and for covering surfaces with material.

Polystyrene adhesives

As polystyrene is eaten away by some spirit-based adhesives buy a glue that is made specially for the purpose.

Spirit-based adhesives

These are quick to dry and are transparent. I would recommend them for collage and hand-made flower making.

Contact adhesives

These are strong and have to be applied to both surfaces which will bond at once when pressed together. They are the best adhesives to use for gluing the supporting stick to a heavy imported seed pod.

Designing a collage

The guidelines are similar to those given for pressed flower pictures. If you are making a large collage it may not be possible to have extra background material to use in a trial run. However, do have a simulated background on which to practise the design and from which the various pieces may be transferred on to the permanent backing.

Frames and backgrounds

With a picture of what you want to do in your mind, choose a background material which will suit your design: a heavily textured backing would spoil a lacy, lightweight pattern but would be entirely in keeping with bold shapes.

There are two ways of preparing the backing:

❋ Nail together 5cm × 2·5cm (2 in × 1 in) strips of wood (obtainable from do-it-yourself shops) to form a frame. Then stretch

the material tightly across the back of the frame and secure with drawing pins, tacks or a staple gun. The edge may be treated with a covering of braid or carpet webbing. Make certain the thread of the fabric is parallel with the sides of the frame or boards. It must be stretched very taut.

❊❊ Cut the backing material 4cm ($1\frac{1}{2}$in) longer than the chosen piece of hardboard, plywood, or thick cardboard. With the material wrong-side upwards on a flat surface, place the hardboard on to it. Stretch the material and glue to the wrong side of the board mitreing. Again make sure the threads are parallel and the material taut. This covered board may act as a mount for a second, smaller covered board.

Hanging the collage

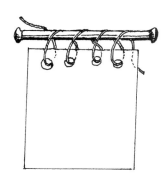

There are several different methods which can be used for hanging the collage:

❊ Leave an extra 10cm (4in) of material at the top of the board when it is covered. Turn this material in and stitch firmly and neatly to make a slot for a piece of dowelling rod. The ends of the dowelling look well finished with small door knobs (from do-it-yourself shops) and the whole painted to tone with the colour scheme.

❊ Cord or braid can be looped through the background and around the rod.

❊ Two loops of material can be made at the top of the collage for a rod.

❊ Hardboard will take small picture screws and rings.

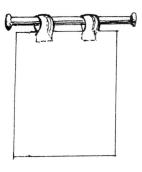

Methods of hanging a collage

Collages made on covered boards can be framed either simply by yourself (the shop will cut the wood to your measurements) or professionally. Glazing detracts from their three-dimensional quality. Keep them free from dust with a feather duster.

Collages do not have to be permanent. They are not expensive to make and the pleasure from the making should not be underestimated. If you do have frames made for your work, they can be used again and again with a different design on a new backing. I think perhaps we tend to cling too long to our handiwork.

Seed collage

These designs call for great accuracy and it is often necessary to use graph paper for the initial plotting of the pattern. Then, with tracing paper, transfer the design to the chosen background material. The material must be kept constantly taut over a backing of strong card, plywood or hardboard.

A seed picture made on a 30cm
(12in) plywood base, and outlined
with gold and silver cord. The
seeds used are lentil, mustard,
peppercorn, split pea and linseed,
and the design is decorated with
poppy seed head tops
Arranger: Joyce Monks

Any seeds that will contribute form, colour and texture can be
used, including the following:
Acanthus (brown and shiny)
Angelica
Barley (cream)
Helipterum (cream and fluffy)
Hollyhock
Lavatera
Melon (cream)
Oat (cream)
Sunflower
Vegetable marrow (cream)
Wheat (cream)

The inspiration for this seed
collage came from a Wedgwood
plate. The large seeds forming the
circles came from an old seed
necklace; the others are melon
seeds. The dragons were outlined
in wool and filled in with bird seed.
The material in the centre was
dried in a desiccant
*Arranger: Inge Hanford, in memory
of her late husband*

8

Flowers for Special Occasions

Special occasions must have special flowers. We use them all the time, not only to celebrate, to express love and sympathy, but to give our homes life.

It is true that special flowers are nearly always fresh, but there are some roles that dried plant material fulfils more easily, and silk flowers, as I have mentioned before, are often chosen for an event simply because they can be kept as mementos.

Garlands

The word garland suggests celebrations. Used by the Ancient Greeks for every festive event and later adopted by the Romans, they were commonplace in Renaissance Italy to mark high days and holy days. Perhaps to us they call to mind the delicate reliefs of Robert Adam. They have an engaging aura of spontaneity about them.

At Christmas you could have glittering garlands dressing the chimney-piece, surrounding the door cases and decking the staircase. You could equally well have garlands of wired natural plant material which are enduring enough to be stored and brought out on important occasions. A garlanded table is a lovely sight at a party and far easier to achieve with preserved material, with the addition of a few silk flowers if wished, than a fresh table garland, for the mechanics for the latter are heavy and moist. A garland can also be arranged in a zigzag down the centre of a long table.

Hazel nuts and walnuts wired and
used amongst the cream and
brown glycerined leaves in a table
decoration. The flowers are silk,
peach-coloured and soft blue

Long-lasting, wired garlands of natural plant material

Each leaf, cone or seed head (and silk flowers, if wished) should be wired and taped individually before being assembled on to a 'backbone' of taped strong wire. I find two 35·5cm (14in) 18 gauge wires the easiest to handle. It is less cumbersome to add extra 'backbone' wire as it becomes necessary than to start off with an unmanageable long length.

The separate pieces, neatly taped, adhere readily to the sticky taped 'backbone' but are further strengthened by an additional twist or two of tape. Wire is necessary for heavy items, e.g. large cones, jacarana pods or similar weighty plant material. The garland should be neat and flat at the back with the plant material placed to the front of the 'backbone', radiating sideways and outwards. The advantage of this method is that each leaf or seed head may be precisely positioned which is not always possible when more complicated mechanics have to be concealed.

The finished garland is very pliable and may be looped, wound round a pillar or simply hung vertically. Choose a good background for the garland which will enhance the well spaced plant material, with every individual piece showing clearly.

Ribboned garlands

This is a very pretty way to decorate the fall of a table cloth.

Tape enough small posies to surround the cloth at intervals of 30–35cm (12–14in). The spaces between the posies are linked with velvet ribbon.

Swags

Swags are reminiscent of the intricate wood carvings of Grinling Gibbons. A swag may be looped and have drops either end, or it can be hung vertically. Unlike a garland, which can be extremely long, entwining an entire column, the swag's length is limited. They are very enjoyable to make for there is a boundless assortment of material to be had and great scope for interesting grouping and varied outline. Aim for a good feeling of depth. The finished swag may be protected by a clear varnish, left in its natural state or, for Christmas decoration, sprayed gold or silver. If it is lightly touched with spray the contours of the plant material are pleasingly emphasized.

The same method may be employed for making a swag as for

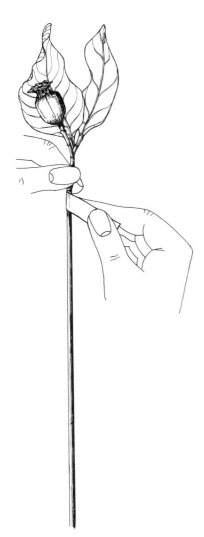

Taping individual pieces to the 'backbone' wire for a garland

These posies can be made up and
stored until you need to decorate
the fall of a table cloth quickly.
They are made with acrocliniums,
glycerined eucalyptus and beech
together with a few silk lilies of the
valley. They are linked around the
table with rose-coloured velvet
ribbon and carefully pinned to the
pale pink cloth

making a wired garland except for two points: the flow of plant material will be slightly downwards for the vertical swag and towards the centre of the curve, from either end, for the looped swag, and some pieces of plant material will need longer wired stems in order to create greater width. Because of the extra width it may be necessary to wire the individual pieces on to the 'backbone' more often, especially if they are weighty. A thin cane, of the kind sold to support pot plants, or a length of 6mm × 6mm ($\frac{1}{4}$in × $\frac{1}{4}$in) strip wood, taped as you would tape 18 gauge wire, also makes a firm 'backbone' for a wired swag or garland to be hung vertically.

Peg board can be used as a base for a vertical swag. The wired ends of the pieces of plant material are pushed through the holes and secured. Avoid the flat look these mechanics produce by having longer stemmed pieces down the centre so that you achieve an attractively curved contour. Two or three or more separate pieces of peg board can be wired to a length of dowelling rod, leaving a space between each bit of peg board. Back each length of peg board with soft material to prevent the wires scratching the surface on which the swag is hung.

Petite arrangements

These small arrangements are included in this chapter because they make such good presents. Little arrangements between 10cm (4in) and 23cm (9in) are 'petite'; under 10cm (4in) they are classed as 'miniature'. The petite size is so portable that it makes a practical gift, especially for a friend in hospital. Such a small dried posy will not be whisked away at night time, fade or take up valuable room on a locker top. Collect pots and baskets for this purpose, or paint yoghurt cartons in neutral colours so that you always have a container ready for use when needed. A small piece of dried foam fitted snugly into the carton or wired to the base of the basket is the only mechanic needed. Matching petite arrangements make attractive table decorations for a party and can be given as presents to the guests.

The tiny miniature is more of a challenge than the petite because the scale of flower and leaf must be so miniscule. Shells, bottle tops and thimbles are commonly used as containers.

A wired swag containing various seed heads and glycerined material

The mechanics for this unusual swag are dry foam on pieces of hardboard, attached to lengths of wood. Protea flowers form a focal point in each group. Many kinds of nuts and seed pods have been used and the colour runs from cream through all the possible tones and shades of brown. The finished swag has been treated with polyurethane varnish
Arranger: Margaret Noble

The miniature on the right is an interpretative one, with the title 'Half a sixpence'. At the base of the column can be seen half a sixpence, and the arrangement is on a Pearly Queen's hat. The tiny plant material in the brooch is on a pink background. On the left is an all gold triangle against a blue backing. The petite arrangement at the rear uses naturally dried leaves and seed heads with a few silk flowers. The coin (2cm − ¾in diameter) gives the scale
Arranger: Dorothy Gray

OPPOSITE A group of easily made Christmas or party trees

Decorative trees

Decorative trees can be of any height but if they are to be used for table decoration 20cm (8 in) is tall enough. If they are to be placed in other positions in the home they can be considerably bigger. There are two ways of supporting the trees, either by giving them a plaster foot which simulates a mound of soil or by using a fabric-covered pot of a suitable size. The pot should first be half filled with sand and then topped up with plaster into which the 'trunk' is inserted.

It is possible to buy polystyrene cones to decorate and turn into small symmetrical trees. Give these cones a garden cane for a trunk and fix the cane in a plaster-filled, fabric-covered pot. Use a polystyrene adhesive to glue on the decorations.

A stripped branch of tortuoso willow may be held either in a pot or plaster foot. It can be sprayed with a metallic car spray or left natural. Decorate for Christmas with icicles, tinsel and small baubles.

A sparkling tree

To make a glittering tree 60cm (2 feet) high, you will need:
    Five branch-like pieces of plastic glitter foliage
    White florists' tape
    Six 30·5cm (12in) 18 gauge wires
    Reel wire of approximately 30 gauge
    A little cotton wool for padding the trunk
    Paint, the same colour as the branches, for the trunk and plaster

✻   None of the pieces of plastic will be used whole. Select a good top for the tree and cut the branches into natural-looking lengths.

✻✻   Tape an 18 gauge wire for the top of the trunk, and wire and tape each branch before fixing it to the trunk. When the top third of the tree is complete, introduce two more strong taped trunk wires. When all the branches are in position add an 18 gauge wire of suitable length to bring the tree to the required height.

✻✻✻   To ensure that the tree will stand firmly make a 'claw' of the remaining wire. Pad the trunk with cotton wool and tape firmly. Place the wire 'claw' on to a shaped piece of strong card, large enough to balance the height of the tree, and surround it with plaster.

✻✻✻✻   When the plaster is dry paint all the taped and plastered portions. Alternatively fix the trunk into a covered plaster-filled pot.

The *Statice dumosum* tree

Statice dumosum is seen on sale in abundance during the autumn and winter. It is inexpensive and one bunch will make a tree of about 23cm (9in) in height. This statice produces curved spikes densely covered with tiny white flowers. The tree is made in the same way as the sparkling plastic tree. Suitable pieces are selected from the bunch, wired, taped and assembled. The 18 gauge wires used for the trunk, if slightly curved, make the tree more realistic and graceful. Pad the trunk, give the tree 'claws' and a plaster base. You can spray the tree when it is finished with silver or gold and wire artificial holly berries to the branches to resemble hanging fruit.

Large cone trees

Drill a hole in the base of the cone and insert the sharpened end of a thin garden cane or strip wood 6mm × 6mm ($\frac{1}{4} \times \frac{1}{4}$in). Fix the trunk in a covered, plaster-filled pot. Spray the fir cones and glitter them for Christmas decoration. They also look attractive covered with artificial snow.

1 A group which shows the warm side of the colour circle to great advantage.
Textural interest is gained by the use of the glazed pots, the fibre mat base and
the indirect line of garlic bulbs running through the design. The plant material
used is aspidistra, *Grevillea robusta, Ruscus aculeatus, R. hypoglossum, Mahonia
bealei,* small proteas, delphinium seed heads and pressed bracken. The
mechanics are dry foam on a heavy foam holder in the larger of the two brown
painted tins, and a pinholder in the smaller tin used for the second placement.
Arranger: Mary Patterson

2 A colourful Christmas buffet arrangement of silk flowers in a Victorian candelabrum. Ferns, ivy, carnations, poinsettias and forsythia have been combined with velvet fruits, artificial grapes and ribbon bows. *Arranger: Beryl Gray*

3 The flowers here were dried in a desiccant and include some from each season of the year: snowdrops, tulips, narcissi, crocuses, roses, cornflowers, marigolds and montbretia; there are also flowering pieces of *Viburnum tinus*, escallonia, *Philadelphus lemoinei* and *Exochorda giraldii*. The foliage is senecio and *Eleagnus pungens* 'Maculata'. All the material was wired before it was dried and is fixed in dry foam anchored on a 'frog'. The dome has been put behind the flowers for the purpose of photographing the arrangement. *Arranger: Jean Robinson*

4 A bronze urn holding a mixture of dried and glycerined English garden plants. The mechanics are dry foam on a large dry foam holder which gives plenty of base weight. The pale outline material is Solomon's seal and other glycerined plants are *Molucella laevis,* ferns and *Alchemilla mollis.* The dried flowers include greenish heads of hydrangea, *Achillea filipendulina* 'Coronation Gold' and *Helichrysum bracteatum,* bunched in order to make a greater impact. The arrangement stands in the morning room at Sutton Park, near York, the house of Mrs Reginald Sheffield. The colours used in the urn harmonize well with the portrait and the panelling

5 A decoration for a circular dining table presents four interesting sides to the diners. The silk Chinese place-mats create the colour scheme of turquoise and coral which links with the aquamarine cloth and shrimp linen napkins. The mechanics are dry foam anchored to a pinholder for ballast and the base is a small silver tray which raises the design and lightens the appearance. The outline is of dried *Tulipa kaufmanniana* seed pods and glycerined seed heads of Venus fishing rod; these, together with the bead-like seeds of *Dierama pendulum*, create movement in an otherwise static arrangement. Small 'clocks' of a dried compositae daisy, skeletonized *Magnolia grandiflora* and the thistle-like heads of the cardoon *Cynara cardunculus* give an ethereal note. Strength is supplied by the solid forms of dried gourds, the shiny fruits of the raffia palm, the compact heads of a species of protea and large papery rods of *Cardiospermum halicacabum*. *Arranger: George Smith*

6 These delicate pressed pictures are mounted on silk. The leaves in the left-hand one are acer and *Alchemilla alpina*, the tendrils those of the Passion flower. The flowers are from Potentilla 'Gibson's Scarlet' and *Hydrangea paniculata*. The right-hand picture has astilbe leaves, tendrils from a cucumber plant, wild rose flowers, *Hydrangea paniculata* and the rose 'Ballerina'.
Arranger: Jean Revitt

Topiary tree

You will need:
    46cm (18in) of dowelling rod
    A 10cm (4in) flower pot
    Reel wire
    A 10cm (4in) plastic foam block
    A small piece of chicken wire to cover the foam

❋   Drill two small holes through the dowelling rod, one 2·5cm (1in) the other 11·5cm (4½in) from an end. This end is the top of the tree.

❋❋   Fix the rod into the pot with plaster and allow it to set hard.

❋❋❋   Push the dowelling rod through the centre of the block of plastic foam to a position just below the top hole and just above the bottom one.

❋❋❋❋   Surround the foam with a piece of 2·5cm (1in) chicken wire. Thread two lengths of reel wire through the holes and secure the chicken wire to the rod with them, preventing the foam from slipping down the dowelling.

There are many variations of this tree which will stand about 56cm (18in) when finished. It may be made up using fresh flowers and foliage (in which case wrap soaked foam in cling foil before impaling it on the rod), preserved or plastic plant material. Several trees make an attractive buffet table decoration.

Nut ring

You will need:
    A circle of strong card, outer radius 14cm (5½in), inner radius 7·5cm (3in)
    22 spring clip wooden clothes pegs, or:
    18 dolly pegs, or:
    22 6mm × 6mm (¼in × ¼in) neatly cut lengths of strip wood 7·5cm (3in) long
    The wooden pegs or lengths of wood make the edge.

❋   Cut the card into a ring and glue on the pegs at carefully measured intervals.

❋❋   When the pegs have set fast, mix enough plaster to cover one-third of the ring and place cones, nuts and seed heads into it before it hardens. Continue until the ring is completed.

A nut ring. This one has been sprayed lightly with gold, but it would also look attractive left in its natural state

A very tall, heavy piece of wood which could be used in a children's corner

'Nativity' displays the beauty of stripped tortuoso willow. The flowers are made from honesty and there are a few skeletonized leaves with some dried ballota in the simple arrangement, which has been fixed in plaster

❋❋❋   When the plaster is quite firm, more nuts can be stuck on in order to give height.

❋❋❋❋   The finished decoration may be sprayed with a metallic aerosol or left in its natural state.

Plaster as a mechanic

For any arrangement of dried and glycerined material that is to be used occasionally and then stored away, plaster holds the stems very securely and nothing is loosened by movement as sometimes happens with dry foam. Very little plaster is needed and this may either be put into the container or on to a piece of card cut to size. The plaster should be painted to merge with the plant material.

Church flowers

A church festival nearly always gives the opportunity for some preserved designs. Bookmarks for the choir pews and lectern, made from petersham ribbon and decorated with dried, glycerined and skeletonized materials, are usually in evidence.

For the week-by-week arrangements in a church the biscuit-hued stone walls are not the ideal background for similar coloured plant material. Some churches and cathedrals like to have dried arrangements during the winter months when fresh flowers are very expensive. These arrangements, often pedestals, should be positioned in a good light and if possible with a contrasting background. Modern church buildings have plain white or coloured walls and these act as a foil for the monochromatic beige pedestal. Shapes chosen for these designs should be bold, clean and unfussy.

Where there is a children's corner it is rewarding to give them a special place for their flowers. All small children enjoy doing flowers. A really tall and weighty piece of dried wood, composed if necessary of several pieces joined together on a good solid base piece, makes an interesting and naturalistic area for flowers. It also enables several children to contribute their offerings. Two tins and wire netting will be needed for base placements and plenty of platforms, at different heights on the dried wood structure, made for other simple containers. Decked with flowers, the 'tree' is festive and very attractive. It is also a way of teaching the young about balance, scale and proportion.

Table arrangements

Table arrangements surely take the leading role amongst special-occasion flowers.

A buffet table adorned with a tall, striking design and with a matching garland skirting it is a delight to see. But the formal dinner party decoration gives great scope for originality and is for me one of the most pleasurable areas for arranging flowers. The combination of flowers, candles, good food, wine and friends is one of the happiest. Can you imagine not having flowers at such times?

Because a table arrangement is seen from very close to, it should be perfect. The height should not obscure the view the diners have of each other. Candles are made to be lit and should stand clear of plant material for the sake of safety.

A few made-up table decorations kept carefully in polythene and ready to whisk out for unexpected guests are splendid morale boosters, for they will turn an improvised meal into a party.

Fruit

Fruit has always been used for table decoration; the variety of colour, texture and form is exquisite. The ancient Egyptians and Greeks appreciated the beauty of it and most of us have seen paintings, television plays and films of imaginary Roman banquets in which piles of fruit adorn the feast.

For those without a garden an arrangement of fruit is an excellent substitute for flowers, especially if a basket or some unusual dish is used as a container. A small tin of water plus a pinholder may be hidden amongst the fruit for the odd few fresh leaves and flowers, but if there are none to hand add some glycerined or silk flowers and foliage.

Plastic and porcelain fruit is obtainable and plastic grapes come top of my list of artificial fruit for they are difficult to distinguish from the real ones. They are also manufactured in every colour and are compulsively collectable. The gold, bronze, silver and glass ones are particularly valuable for Christmas arrangements. Dried gourds, sprayed or painted if you like, and artichokes, are bold in form and contrast well with bunches of grapes.

Remember that plastic flowers and fruit are not allowed in show work. In our own homes however, we may enjoy whatever gives us pleasure, and this is what matters – the realization that it is possible to be an artist with flowers. At least half the fun of flower arranging lies in experimenting, so do have an open mind about modern designs, silk flowers and the use of paint and dried wood. Try everything, for the permutations are limitless. If you are a lover of the traditional, think of making a *decoration* rather than a flower

Fresh apples and pears, plastic grapes and some pieces of *Cardiospermum halicacabum* (balloon vine) combine with one silk rose to form a pleasing group in a deep green fruit dish

arrangement; I think it helps those who only like fresh flowers to approach preserved material this way. It is an advantage that flower arranging is so impermanent – we can try again tomorrow.

Glossary

Abstract A style of arrangement which uses plant material for its design qualities and not naturalistically.

Accessory Anything other than plant material, container, base, background or drape, used as part of an exhibit.

Base A stand under the container.

Biennial A plant that needs two growing seasons to complete its life cycle.

Bract A modified leaf, often as colourful as a petal.

Calyx The outer part of a flower which protects the petals and consists of sepals. It is usually green.

Conditioning The term given to the treatment of flowers and foliage of various stem types after cutting and before arranging.

Container Used to be called vase and refers to anything into which flowers are put.

Design A flower arrangement with or without an accessory.

Design elements The working qualities of colour, line, form, texture and space.

Design principles The guidelines to the use of the elements: balance, rhythm, dominance, contrast, scale and proportion.

Exhibit The term in the show schedule for the entire design.

Floral foam One of the main mechanics for the flower arranger. There are two main sorts of foam: green for soaking in water for fresh plant material and brown for dried and wired stems.

Floret A small flower, part of a large head or cluster.

Foam holder Similar to a pinholder but with only a few strong pins on to which the foam is anchored. The best are made of lead and so give valuable base weight.

Focal point An area of greater interest in an arrangement, usually near the centre of the design.

Frog A small lightweight three-pronged foam holder.

Garland An elongated and flexible design that may be twined round a pillar, hung vertically or looped.

Half-hardy annual A plant which completes its life cycle in one growing season but needs protection until frost danger is past.

Hardy annual A plant that germinates, flowers and seeds in one growing season.

Hardy perennial A plant that lives for an indefinite number of years. Not a tree or shrub.

Hogarth curve The lazy S curve extolled by the artist William Hogarth (1697–1764) in his *Analysis of Beauty*.

Inflorescence The arrangement of the flowers on the stem, e.g. a spike (lavender), umbel (allium), corymb (hydrangea), panicle (lilac) etc.

Interpretative design An arrangement portraying a title. Plant material and other components all help to illustrate the theme.

Landscape A design interpreting a natural scene, e.g. moorland, woodland, waterside etc.

Mechanics The various means by which stems are held in position.

Natural plant material Either fresh or preserved material.

Pinholder An indispensable mechanic – a Japanese-inspired, lead-based, brass-pinned stem holder.

Swag A three-dimensional design of plant material assembled with no visible background.

Suppliers

Cards and calendars

Flower Hobbies
T. J. Sharpe Printers Ltd
Old Mill Industrial Estate
Mill Lane
Fazeley
Tamworth Staffordshire B78 3QB
Mail order service

Impress
Slough Farm
Westhall
Hailsworth Suffolk
*Mail order service: greetings cards and
other materials for pressed flower work*

Flower arranging aids and accessories

Clive Brooker
Stanmore Pottery
10 York Avenue
Stanmore Middlesex HA7 2HS
Modern containers

The Diddy Box
The Nurseries
Pinchback
Spalding Lincolnshire PE11 3XY

Joyce Withy
Bumbles Moreton Road
Ongar Essex
Containers

Frames and Mounts

Lebro Frames
St Luke's Buildings
5–8 Hart Street Bridge
Southport Merseyside
*Frames and mounts for pressed flowers including
Victorian-style velvet frames*

Cullen Picture Frames
14 Chapel Street
Hambleton YO8 9JG

Presses

Branches of Habitat and W.H. Smith & Son Ltd

Seed merchants

Samuel Dobie and Sons Ltd
Upper Dee Mills
Llangollen Clwyd

Suttons Seeds
Hele Road
Torquay Devon

Thompson and Morgan Ltd
London Road
Ipswich Suffolk

W.J. Unwin Ltd
Histon Cambridgeshire

Miscellaneous supplies

Creative Beadcraft Ltd
Unit 26
Chilton Trading Estate
Holmer Green
High Wycombe Buckinghamshire
Mail order; beads etc

Framecraft
262 Rocky Lane
Great Barr
Birmingham B42 1QX
Trinket boxes

Paperchase
213 Tottenham Court Road
London W1
Various decorative papers including double
crepe and crinkle foil

Pretty Things
587 Lichfield Road
Four Oaks
Sutton Coldfield West Midlands
Beads, gold and silver braids etc

77 Bulbridge Road
Wilton
Salisbury Wiltshire SP2 OLE
Flora Seal, a colourless protective aerosol
coating for preserved flowers; also preserving crystals

Strand Glassfibre Ltd
Brentway Trading Estate
Brentford Middlesex
Paperweight casting kits

Index